Editor
Eric Migliaccio

Managing Editor
Ina Massler Levin, M.A.

Editor-in-Chief
Sharon Coan, M.S. Ed.

Cover Art
Barb Lorseyedi

Illustrators
Howard Chaney
Kevin Barnes

Art Manager
Kevin Barnes

Art Director
CJae Froshay

Imaging
James Edward Grace
Rosa C. See

Product Manager
Phil Garcia

Publisher
Mary D. Smith, M.S. Ed.

- Phonemic Awareness
- Phonics
- Fluency
- Vocabulary
- Comprehension

Author

Jodene Lynn Smith, M.A.

Teacher Created Resources, Inc.
6421 Industry Way
Westminster, CA 92683
www.teachercreated.com

ISBN-0-7439-3021-5

©2004 Teacher Created Resources, Inc.

Reprinted, 2005

Made in U.S.A.

Table of Contents

Introduction

Reading and the teaching of reading have always been at the forefront of discussions in education. Recent discussions bear no differences. Some, such as the media, criticize schools for not knowing how to effectively teach reading, and yet we know more today than ever about effective reading instruction. In 2000, the National Reading Panel compiled research reflecting effective reading instruction methodologies. The report titled "Teaching Children to Read: An Evidence-Based Assessment of the Scientific Research Literature on Reading and Its Implications for Reading Instruction—Reports of Subgroups" identifies key elements of reading instruction. The report targets the following five elements of reading instruction:

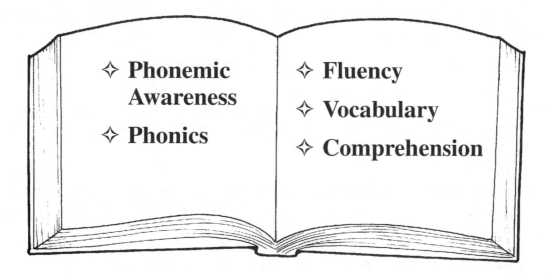

✦ **Phonemic Awareness**

✦ **Phonics**

✦ **Fluency**

✦ **Vocabulary**

✦ **Comprehension**

This book has been designed to assist the classroom teacher with strategies appropriate for teaching the elements of reading identified by the National Reading Panel. The book is divided into five sections appropriately named after each of the elements of reading instruction. Within each section, you will find a definition of the element of reading, as well as a variety of ways to implement these keys of effective reading instruction in your classroom. Some of the activities are teacher-directed activities, while others are games that students can use for practice. A few student activity sheets are provided when appropriate, which can be copied and distributed for the students to complete.

The activities included in this book are not meant to be a complete reading program. Your school probably has already adopted a reading program. The activities in this book are meant to provide you with ideas of ways you can make teaching the elements of reading more fun.

Meeting Reading Standards

You will notice that the following listing of reading standards encompasses more than the key elements of reading instruction identified by the National Reading Panel; however, some of the standards below are either implied within the elements of reading or are critical to the success of teaching reading. For example, although concepts of print are not a specific element listed by the National Reading Panel, children need to have an understanding of how our print system works in order to begin reading.

1. The student understands and uses concepts of print in reading texts.

   A. The student identifies parts of a book, including the front cover, back cover, title, and author of a book.

   B. The student understands that printed materials convey information.

   C. The student reads words from left to right and from top to bottom.

   D. The student identifies and names all uppercase and lowercase letters.

   E. The student recognizes individual letters.

   F. The student recognizes that words are composed of letters.

   G. The student recognizes that sentences are composed of separate words.

2. The student recognizes and manipulates sounds in spoken language.

   A. The student identifies individual sounds in a word. (Phoneme isolation)

   B. The student recognizes the same sounds in different words. (Phoneme identity)

   C. The student identifies a word in a set of words that does not have the same phoneme. (Phoneme categorization)

   D. The student blends separate phonemes into one word. (Phoneme blending)

   E. The student segments a word into its individual phonemes. (Phoneme segmentation)

   F. The student deletes a phoneme to identify a new word. (Phoneme deletion)

   G. The student adds a phoneme to create a new word. (Phoneme addition)

   H. The student substitutes phonemes to create new words. (Phoneme substitution)

Meeting Reading Standards (cont.)

3. The student recognizes and manipulates sounds in written language.

    A. The student recognizes and produces corresponding letters and sounds.

    B. The student understands that as letters of words change, so do the sounds.

    C. The student reads CV, VC, and CVC words. (V = vowel, C = consonant)

    D. The student decodes unknown words using basic elements of phonetic analysis and structural analysis.

    E. The student applies phonemic awareness skills to reading.

4. The student recognizes sounds and rhythms of language.

    A. The student recognizes high-frequency sight words.

    B. The students recites poetry with appropriate rhythm and expression.

    C. The student distinguishes between appropriate and inappropriate rhythm and expression.

5. The student develops a deeper understanding of word usage.

    A. The student recognizes and categorizes words.

    B. The student describes objects and events.

    C. The student develops a broader understanding of a word through its use in various contexts.

    D. The student determines the correct word meaning of multiple-meaning words in context.

    E. The student uses context to resolve ambiguities about word and sentence meaning.

6. The student applies variety of strategies to enhance comprehension.

    A. The student uses pictures and content to make predictions.

    B. The student makes connections between prior knowledge and text.

    C. The student asks and answers questions about the text.

    D. The student modifies existing knowledge based on new concepts encountered in reading materials.

    E. The student applies reading materials to a real-life situation.

    F. The student monitors comprehension while reading and asks questions to clarify understanding.

    G. The student can ask questions and support answers by connecting prior knowledge with information found in and inferred from text.

Meeting Reading Standards (cont.)

7. **The student demonstrates competence in the general skills and strategies for reading a variety of literary texts.**

    A. The student applies reading skills and strategies to a variety of literary passages and texts.

    B. The student identifies setting, main characters, main events, and problems in stories.

    C. The student makes simple inferences regarding the order of events and possible outcomes.

    D. The student identifies the main ideas or theme of a story.

    E. The student relates stories to personal experiences.

8. **The student understands structural patterns and organizations in texts.**

    A. The student recognizes chronological order.

    B. The student recognizes logical order.

    C. The student recognizes sequential order.

    D. The student identifies setting, main characters, main events, and problems in stories.

9. **The student draws conclusions and makes inferences about texts.**

    A. The student raises questions.

    B. The student has reactions.

    C. The student makes observations.

    D. The student makes interpretations.

    E. The student makes predictions.

Phonemic Awareness

Phonemic awareness is students' awareness of the sounds in language and how those sounds work together to form words. The word *phonemic* comes from the word *phoneme*, which relates to individual sounds. The /s/ in *sun* is a phoneme, as are /u/ and /n/. Phonemes are not necessarily isolated to individual letters because phonemes have to do with sounds rather than written letters. In the word *ship*, /sh/ is a phoneme, too. In a narrow sense, phonemic awareness means "sound awareness." In a broader sense, it is a student's ability to recognize, differentiate, and manipulate sounds. The importance of phonemic awareness cannot be understated. There is ample research and evidence that shows that phonemic awareness is a strong predictor of a student's reading success.

Phonemic awareness is developed in several ways. Prior to coming to school, many students gain phonemic awareness through their environments either at home or in preschool or both. In any of these cases, phonemic awareness was probably not directly taught but rather absorbed through a language-rich environment. Most likely, students sang songs, recited nursery rhymes, read books, made up riddles, and began playing with language on their own. Because of the students' extensive and varied experiences with language, phonemic awareness was developed. Given the fact that students become phonemically aware in many different ways, it is important to keep in mind that although this section of the book focuses on various ways to directly and explicitly develop phonemic awareness, creating a language-rich classroom environment is crucial.

There are many students for whom phonemic awareness must be directly and explicitly taught. These students either did not have the experiences mentioned above or did not "absorb" them in such a way as to develop phonemic awareness. The good news is there is evidence that phonemic awareness can be taught. The table below lists eight types of activities that can be used for phonemic awareness instruction, practice, and assessment.

1. **Phoneme Isolation** (*beginning on page 13*)

2. **Phoneme Identity** (*beginning on page 18*)

3. **Phoneme Categorization** (*beginning on page 23*)

4. **Phoneme Blending** (*beginning on page 30*)

5. **Phoneme Segmentation** (*beginning on page 35*)

6. **Phoneme Deletion** (*beginning on page 38*)

7. **Phoneme Addition** (*beginning on page 40*)

8. **Phoneme Substitution** (*beginning on page 41*)

Phonemic Awareness (cont.)

Provided in this section are examples of each type of phonemic-awareness activity. The first page of each activity provides a description and example of the activity. The following pages (if applicable) provide a variety of ways in which the task can be applied, practiced, or adapted.

Phonemic awareness activities are well suited for whole-class lessons, as language warm-ups in small-group lessons, or for that five minutes that remain before the recess bell rings. Be sure that when you present a new activity, you provide sufficient time to both model and practice the activity.

Oral vs. Written

The activities provided on the pages within this section provide oral examples. For students who are ready, any of the activities can be extended. By writing down the sounds or words that students are manipulating, students begin to see the letter/sound relationships in the activities. Depending on students' abilities you may wish to write the letters yourself on the whiteboard or have the students write the letters using a paper and pencil or small chalkboards and chalk. Developing students' awareness of how the letters and sounds work together will help them in both reading and spelling.

Assessing Phonemic Awareness

Provided on pages 10–12 is a phonemic awareness assessment. This assessment tool can be used to determine areas in which students need additional instruction and practice. Photocopy one assessment per child. The assessment is given one-on-one. Directions for each task are provided in each section of the assessment. Write down student responses on the lines provided and record the scores for each section in the summary box on the front page.

There are five points possible for each type of activity. A score of four or five indicates a student is competent in performing that particular phonemic awareness activity. A score of less than four indicates the student needs additional instruction or practice.

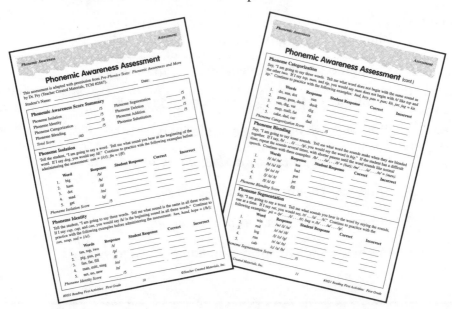

Modeling Phonemic Awareness

Many students develop phonemic awareness before any formal phonemic awareness activities are introduced in school. Students who have rich language backgrounds may already be skilled in many phonemic awareness activities. However, there are many students for whom direct, explicit phonemic awareness instruction will be necessary. For these students, modeling is crucial.

Model phonemic awareness activities by talking through and demonstrating for students how to complete a task, step by step. Next, have students complete the activity by repeating what you have said. Then, complete the activity together. Finally, have the students complete the activity alone. Once students have demonstrated their ability with the word being analyzed, provide another word on which they can try the same activity. The example below is a phoneme segmentation activity; however, the format can be used to model any of the phonemic awareness activities.

Teacher: I am going to say a word. I want you to listen as I say all the sounds I hear in the word. The word is *red*: /r/ . . . /e/ . . . /d/. Now, this time, I want you to repeat the sounds after I say them. /r/. . . /e/ . . . /d/

Students: /r/ . . . /e/ . . . /d/

Teacher: Now, let's say the sounds in the word *red* together.

Everyone: /r/ . . . /e/ . . . /d/

Teacher: Now you say the sounds in the word *red* by yourselves.

Students: /r/ . . . /e/ . . . /d/

Teacher: Excellent, now let's do the same thing with the word *bug*.

Some students will need you to model this activity a few times until they become familiar with the task. Other students will require you to do extensive modeling as they learn about how sounds work together to make words. Even when students are familiar with a particular task, you may want to again model if you change the task slightly—such as by adding words with more sounds—or if students need assistance because they are having a difficult time with a word.

Phonemic Awareness Assessment

This assessment is adapted with permission from *Pre-Phonics Tests: Phonemic Awareness and More* by Dr. Fry (Teacher Created Resources, TCM #2667).

Student's Name: _____ Date: _____

Phonemic Awareness Score Summary

Phoneme Isolation	_____ /5	Phoneme Segmentation	_____ /5
Phoneme Identity	_____ /5	Phoneme Deletion	_____ /5
Phoneme Categorization	_____ /5	Phoneme Addition	_____ /5
Phoneme Blending	_____ /5	Phoneme Substitution	_____ /5
Total Score	_____ /40		

Phoneme Isolation

Tell the student, "I am going to say a word. Tell me what sound you hear at the beginning of the word. If I say *dog*, you would say /d/." Continue to practice with the following examples before administering the assessment: *can = (/c/); fin = (/f/).*

	Word	Response	Student Response	Correct	Incorrect
1.	big	/b/	_____	_____	_____
2.	ham	/h/	_____	_____	_____
3.	dot	/d/	_____	_____	_____
4.	mad	/m/	_____	_____	_____
5.	get	/g/	_____	_____	_____

Phoneme Isolation Score _____ /5

Phoneme Identity

Tell the student, "I am going to say three words. Tell me what sound is the same in all three words. If I say *cup, cap,* and *can*, you would say /k/ is the beginning sound in all three words." Continue to practice with the following examples before administering the assessment: *hen, hand, hope = (/h/); sun, soup, sad = (/s/).*

	Words	Response	Student Response	Correct	Incorrect
1.	tan, top, two	/t/	_____	_____	_____
2.	pig, pan, pot	/p/	_____	_____	_____
3.	fan, far, fill	/f/	_____	_____	_____
4.	man, mitt, mug	/m/	_____	_____	_____
5.	net, no, new	/n/	_____	_____	_____

Phoneme Identity Score _____ /5

Phonemic Awareness Assessment (cont.)

Phoneme Categorization

Say, "I am going to say three words. Tell me what word does not begin with the same sound as the other two. If I say *top, man,* and *tip,* you would say *man* does not begin with /t/ like *top* and *tip.*" Continue to practice with the following examples: *bed, boy, pan = pan; kit, jar, jug = kit.*

	Words	Response	Student Response	Correct	Incorrect
1.	do, sun, dot	sun	_____	_____	_____
2.	game, gum, duck	duck	_____	_____	_____
3.	van, dig, vet	dig	_____	_____	_____
4.	map, mall, fat	fat	_____	_____	_____
5.	cake, dad, car	dad	_____	_____	_____

Phoneme Categorization Score _____ /5

Phoneme Blending

Say, "I am going to say some sounds. Tell me what word the sounds make when they are blended together. If I say, /b/ . . . /i/ . . . /g/, you would say the word is *big.*" If the student has a difficult time, repeat the sounds several times, with shorter pauses until the word sounds like normal speech. Continue with these examples: */b/ . . . /a/ . . . /t/ = (bat); /m/ . . . /e/ . . . /n/ = (men).*

	Words	Response	Student Response	Correct	Incorrect
1.	/t/ /e/ /n/	ten	_____	_____	_____
2.	/b/ /a/ /d/	bad	_____	_____	_____
3.	/p/ /o/ /t/	pot	_____	_____	_____
4.	/j/ /e/ /t/	jet	_____	_____	_____
5.	/f/ /i/ /l/	fill	_____	_____	_____

Phoneme Blending Score _____ /5

Phoneme Segmentation

Say, "I am going to say a word. Tell me what sounds you hear in the word by saying the sounds, one at a time. If I say *rat,* you would say, /r/ ... /a/ ... /t/." Continue to practice with the following examples: *pit = /p/ . . . /i/ . . . /t/; bug = /b/ . . . /u/ . . . /g/.*

	Word	Response	Student Response	Correct	Incorrect
1.	win	/w/ /i/ /n/	_____	_____	_____
2.	red	/r/ /e/ /d/	_____	_____	_____
3.	log	/l/ /o/ /g/	_____	_____	_____
4.	ran	/r/ /a/ /n/	_____	_____	_____
5.	cab	/c/ /a/ /b/	_____	_____	_____

Phoneme Segmentation Score _____ /5

Phonemic Awareness Assessment (cont.)

Phoneme Deletion

Tell the student, "I am going to say a word. Tell me what word is left when you take away the first sound. If I say *bat*, you would take away the /b/ and say the word *at*." Continue to practice with the following examples before administering the assessment: *fan = an; sink = ink.*

Word	Response	Student Response	Correct	Incorrect
1. heat	eat	_____	_____	_____
2. rice	ice	_____	_____	_____
3. sit	it	_____	_____	_____
4. for	or	_____	_____	_____
5. gate	ate	_____	_____	_____

Phoneme Deletion Score _____ /5

Phoneme Addition

Tell the student, "I am going to say a sound and a word. Tell me what new word is made when you put the sound at the beginning of the word. If I say, add /s/ to the beginning of the word *at*, you would say the word *sat*." Continue to practice with the following examples before administering the assessment: *all with /b/ = ball; oil with /s/ = soil*

Word	Sound	Response	Student Response	Correct	Incorrect
1. old	/f/	fold	_____	_____	_____
2. am	/j/	jam	_____	_____	_____
3. as	/h/	has	_____	_____	_____
4. ill	/p/	pill	_____	_____	_____
5. rag	/d/	drag	_____	_____	_____

Phoneme Addition Score _____ /5

Phoneme Substitution

Tell the student, "I am going to say a word and give some directions about what sounds to change. Change the sounds to make a new word. If I say, change the /c/ in *car* to /f/, you would say the word *far*." Continue to practice with the following examples before administering the assessment: *bun (change /b/ for /r/) = run; jet (change /j/ for /l/) = let.*

Word	Sounds	Response	Student Response	Correct	Incorrect
1. fog	change /f/ for /h/	hog	_____	_____	_____
2. ten	change /t/ for /m/	men	_____	_____	_____
3. van	change /v/ for /c/	can	_____	_____	_____
4. hip	change /h/ for /s/	sip	_____	_____	_____
5. hot	change /h/ for /g/	got	_____	_____	_____

Phoneme Substitution Score _____ /5

Phoneme Isolation

Phoneme isolation activities require students to isolate sounds in a word. Beginning phoneme isolation activities should have students isolating initial sounds. For example, ask students, "What sound do you hear at the beginning of the word *cat*?" Students should respond by saying /c/. Continue having students practice phoneme isolation using words from this list:

Word	Response	Word	Response
dog	/d/	kit	/k/
get	/g/	late	/l/
bag	/b/	moon	/m/
to	/t/	net	/n/

Initial-phoneme isolation is fundamental to phonemic awareness activities. Students who have a difficult time isolating the initial phoneme will not be able to manipulate phonemes very successfully. There are many students whose experiences with playing with language may be very limited, and this task may initially be challenging for them. For these students, modeling, followed by practice, is crucial. Model initial phoneme isolation by isolating the beginning of the word from the rest of the word. For example, say to the children, "Listen to the first sound you hear in the word *can*: /k/ . . . /an/. If needed, emphasize the beginning sound again, pausing even longer between the initial sound and the rest of the word. Another way to model isolating initial sounds is to say the initial sound slightly louder than the rest of the word. For example, you may say /k/ loudly and /an/ in a softer voice.

As students become skilled at isolating initial phonemes, they should be challenged with more difficult phoneme isolation activities. See the list and examples below.

✏ **Longer Words**

What sound do you hear at the beginning of the word *cantaloupe*?

✏ **Identify the Ending Phoneme**

What sound do you hear at the end of the word *pat*?

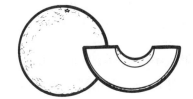

✏ **Identify Medial Phonemes**

What sound do you hear in the middle of the word *pan*?

✏ **Identify Phoneme Position**

Do you hear the /p/ first or last in the word *tap*?

Pages 14 to 17 provide additional practice with phoneme isolation.

Phoneme Isolation Activities

First or Last...or Middle

This activity provides practice isolating initial, ending, and if desired, medial sounds. Students isolate sounds in a word in order to determine the position of the sound—first, last, or medial.

Provide students with manipulatives such as beans or math counters. To begin with, students should have the same number of manipulatives as there are sounds in the word. For example, if there are three sounds in the words you will be practicing, students should have three manipulatives. Students should line up their manipulatives on the floor or table in front of them.

Practice identifying the position of the manipulatives. For example, the first manipulative represents the initial sound of a word. The second manipulative represents the second sound of a word, etc.

Determine the sound for which you want students to listen. Create a list of words. The words on the list should have several with the sound at the beginning of the word, several with the sound at the end of the word, and several with the sound in the middle, if appropriate. For example, if students are going to listen for the /t/ sound, your list may look like this.

Begins with /t/	Ends with /t/
tap	bat
ten	set

Say a word from the list. If students hear /t/ at the beginning of the word, students should slide the first manipulative forward. If students hear /t/ at the end of the word, students should slide the last manipulative forward. For example, if the word is *top*, students would slide the first manipulative forward indicating the /t/ sound is the initial sound. If the word is *mat*, students would slide the last manipulative forward indicating /t/ is the last sound in the word. Demonstrate and practice several examples with students until they understand what is expected.

Silly Sounds

We hear sounds all around us—the bell ringing, water dripping, a fire-engine siren, etc. Have students brainstorm as many sounds they hear on a daily basis. Chart student responses, if desired. Practice isolating the beginning sounds of the sounds. For example, students may say that the recess bell sounds like, "Bzzzzzzzz." Have them isolate the beginning sound /b/. You may also wish to have them isolate the ending sound as well.

Phoneme Isolation Activities (cont.)

Ending to Beginning

Seat students in a circle. Begin play by providing a word, for example, *dot*. The first student must isolate the ending sound of the word *dot* (/t/) and think of a word that begins with that sound (for example, *tap*). The next student must isolate the last sound in *tap* (/p/) and think of a new word that begins with /p/ (for example, *park*). Continue to play around the circle.

Tic, Tack, Sound

Make photocopies of page 16. Four game boards are provided on that page. You may cut the game boards apart and distribute one to each pair of students, or keep the page whole and allow each pair to play four games. The game is played just like Tic, Tack, Toe; however, before a student can place an **X** or **O** on the space, he or she must isolate the beginning sound of the word. The winner must get three in a row. Extend the game by having students isolate the ending or medial sound in the words.

Spin a Word

Photocopy page 17 on index paper and laminate, if desired. Select a student to play first. The student spins the Heads/Tails Spinner to determine if he or she will isolate the beginning or ending sound. Then, he or she spins the Word Spinner to determine the word with which he or she he or she will play. For example, if the student spins heads and the picture of the map, the student would have to isolate the beginning sound of the word *map* (/m/). Play for fun or keep score, if desired.

Blend Isolation

As students become skilled at isolating initial phonemes, challenge them to isolate the initial phoneme on words with blends. For example, say to students, "What is the beginning sound in the word *twin*?" Students should respond by saying /t/. This is an advanced phonemic awareness activity because of the nature of blends. Select words from this list of blends.

bread	plan	slam	smug	spun	swim
clam	play	slap	snack	stay	track
club	scan	sled	snag	sting	tray
flap	skill	slug	snip	stub	twig
grab	skin	small	spot	swam	twin

Tick, Tack, Sound

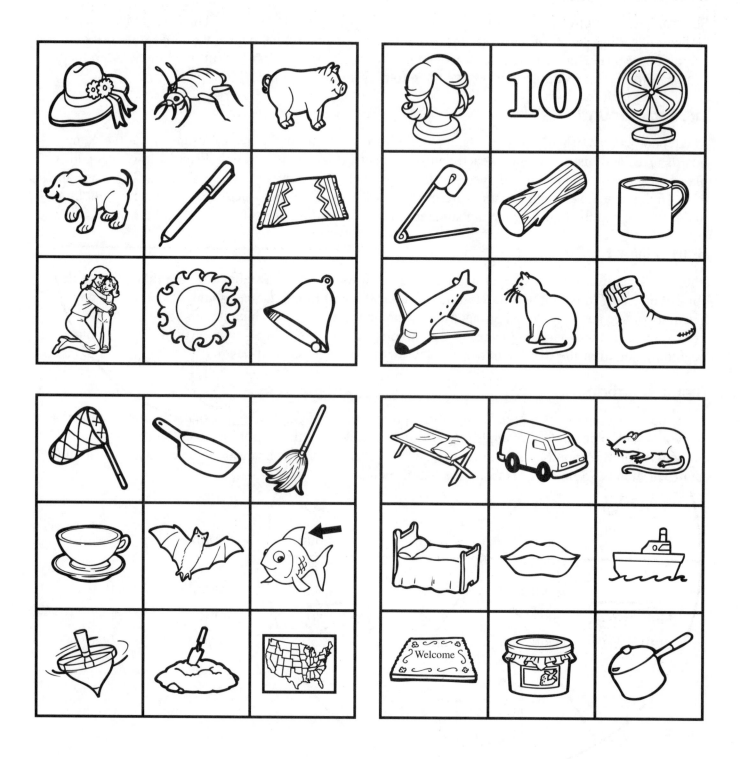

Spin a Word

Directions: Place a paperclip on the **X**. Then, place the tip of a pencil inside the paperclip. Use the paperclip as a spinner. Spin the paperclip around the pencil. The paperclip will act as the pointer.

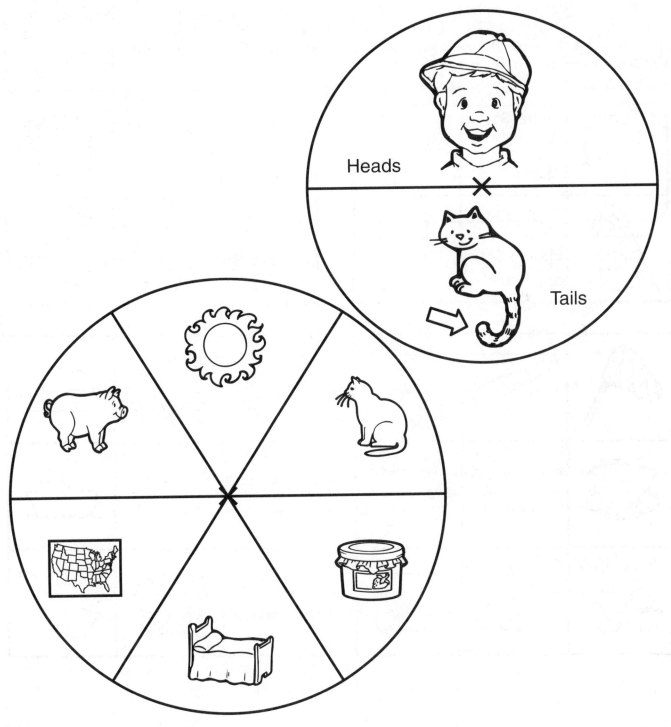

Phoneme Identity Activities

Phoneme identity activities require students to identify the same sound in different words. For example, students should recognize that the /b/ sound is the beginning sound in both *ball* and *bat*.

Same Sound, Three Words

Say three words in a row with the same sound. Students must determine what sound is the same in all three words. To begin, all three words should have the same initial sound. Then, as students become more skilled at this type of activity, say words in which the same sound is at the end of the word. Challenge students who are ready by saying words in which the same sound is in a different position in each word. See the lists below for examples of words.

Initial Sound		
tab, ten, tug	→	/t/
sun, set, say	→	/s/
fan, fat, fill	→	/f/

Medial Sound		
wag, map, zap	→	/a/
pen, jet, bell	→	/e/
mud, bug, nut	→	/u/

Ending Sound		
gum, jam, him	→	/m/
bag, wig, rug	→	/g/
bat, kit, hot	→	/t/

Same Sound in Different Positions		
bad, cub, bat	→	/b/
net, pin, nap	→	/n/
map, dam, mitt	→	/m/

Word Partners

Pair two students. Provide an initial sound for which the students must provide words beginning with the same sound. One student starts and says a word beginning with the target sound. The other student continues by saying a different word beginning with the same sound. For example, if the sound is /d/, the first student may say *dog*, the second student may say *dig*, etc. Students continue providing words until one student cannot think of a word. The student who could not provide a word sits down and a new challenger stands to face the winner. A new sound is given for which this pair must provide words. Adapt this game to ending sounds, if desired.

I'm Going on a Trip

Seat students on the floor in a circle. Begin by selecting a sound you want to target. For example, you may select the /t/ sound. Choose a word beginning with /t/ and say, "I'm going on a trip, and I am packing tape." The student next to you must repeat the item you have said, plus add his or her own item beginning with /t/. For example, "I'm going on a trip and I am packing tape and a tuba." Continue around the circle with each child adding to the list. Try to get all the way around the circle. If a student cannot think of a word beginning with the targeted beginning sound, stop play with that sound and select a new sound.

Phoneme Identity Activities (cont.)

Alliterative Sentences

Identify a target sound, for example, /g/. Students must think of a sentence in which all or most of the words begin with the /g/ sound. For example, a student could come up with the sentence, "Gail the goose goes through the gate." Depending on students' ability levels, it may be helpful to brainstorm words first. Chart the words or a picture for students, if desired. You may also wish to have students draw an illustration of one of the sentences.

Cute Names

Begin by having students isolate the beginning sound of their own name. Then, have them think of another word that describes them and also begins with the same sound as their name. For example, if a student's name was Neil, he could come up with the name "Neat Neil." You may want to have a special day on which students are called their new, cute names all day long. Challenge students to come up with several words that describe themselves and to choose the word they like best; or have students string several words together with their names, such as "Perfectly Peaceful Pete."

Magazine Search

Provide magazines through which students can search for pictures. Provide a target sound for which students will practice. For example, you may ask to students to look for pictures of objects beginning with the same sound as *ball*. Students then search through the magazines for any pictures beginning with /b/. Have students glue the pictures to a piece of chart paper or a large sheet of construction paper. The sheets of construction paper can be assembled into a big book through which students can look. When students are finished, review all the pictures by pointing to each one and having students say its beginning sound and the name of the object. For example, if you point to a ball, students should say, "/b/ . . . ball." You may wish to label each of the pictures with a word.

Beginning Sound Sort

Directions: Cut out the picture cards at the bottom of the page. Say each word. Glue the pictures with the same beginning sound together in a box.

Ending Sound Sort

Directions: Cut out the pictures at the bottom of the page. Say each word and determine the ending sound. Glue each picture next to a picture at the top of the page with the same ending sound.

1.

2.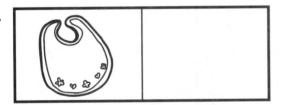

3.

4.

5.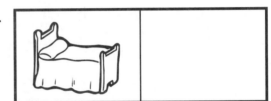

6.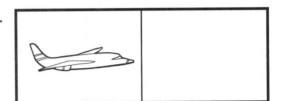

7.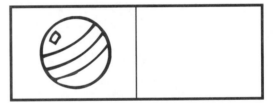

8.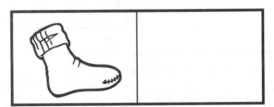

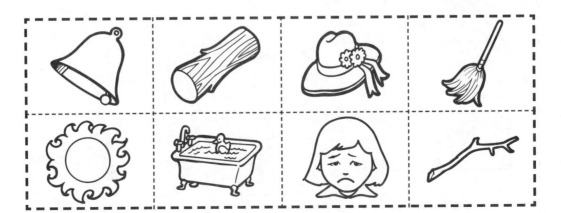

Vowel Sound Sort

Directions: Cut out the pictures at the bottom of the page. Say each word and determine the middle sound. Glue the pictures with the same middle sounds together in a column.

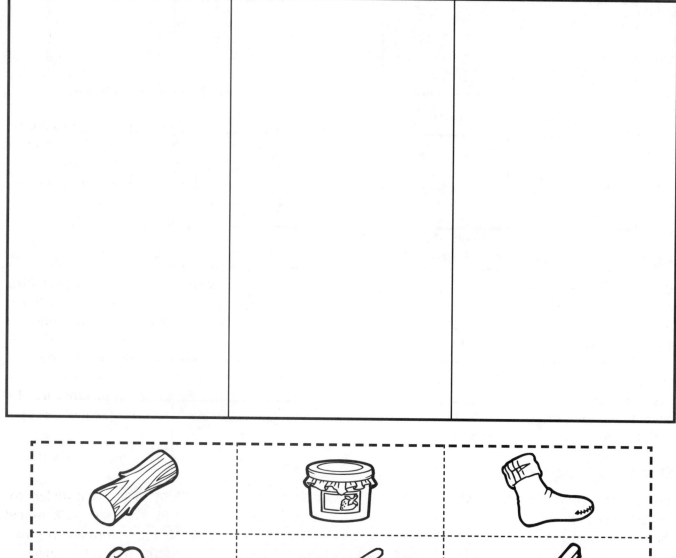

Phoneme Categorization Activities

Phoneme categorization activities require students to see differences and similarities of sounds in words. For example, given a list of three words—*fin, get,* and *fun*—students should be able to identify that *fin* and *fan* begin with the same sound and that *get* begins with a different sound.

Belongs/Doesn't Belong

List three words for students, two of which begin with the same sound and one of which does not. Students must identify the two words that begin with the same sound. For example, if you say the words *hat, bat,* and *hit,* students should identify that the words *hat* and *hit* begin with the same sound. An alternative way to play this game is to have students identify the word that does not belong.

As students become skilled at phoneme categorization, provide more words from which students must select words that belong (or don't belong) based on similar or different sounds. For example, provide a list of five words. Students must select the three words with the same initial sound. Also, challenge students by changing the position of the phonemes that students must categorize. For example, if you say the words *hat, bit,* and *car,* students must tell which word does not have the same ending sound as the other two words.

Animal Categorization

Pages 24–26 contain animal pictures. Each row contains pictures of animals whose names begin with the same sound. Photocopy the pages onto cardstock and color and laminate, if desired. Display four pictures in a pocket chart. Three of the pictures should begin with the same sound. The remaining picture should begin with one of the other sounds. Students should say each word and then identify which pictures go together based on the initial sound. For example, you may place the bat, cat, bee, and bear in the pocket chart. Students should identify that the bat, bear, and bee belong together because they each start with the same beginning sound. Continue displaying groups of picture cards for students to categorize. As students are able, you may wish to have students categorize the pictures by ending sounds or medial sounds as well.

Duck, Dog, Goose

This game is played similarly to "Duck, Duck, Goose." Seat students in a circle. Select one student to be "it." Select a sound on which you want students to focus. The student who is "it" must walk around the outside of the circle. He or she taps each seated child on the head while saying a word that begins with the target sound. For example, the student could say, "Duck, dog, ding, doll." When the student who is "it" says a word beginning with a sound other than the target sound—for example, *goose*—the student who is seated must jump up and chase the student who is "it" around the circle. The student who was "it" must run around the circle and back to the empty space in order to be safe. If the child who was "it" safely returns to the empty space, the other child is now "it." If the child who was "it" is tagged, he or she must be "it" again. Continue play with a different target sound.

Animal Categorization

Animal Categorization (cont.)

Animal Categorization (cont.)

Doesn't Belong

Initial Sounds

Directions: Look at the pictures in each row. Say each word. Cross off the word in each row that does not begin with the same sound as the other two words.

Doesn't Belong (cont.)

Ending Sounds

Directions: Look at the pictures in each row. Say each word. Cross off the word in each row that does not end with the same sound as the other two words.

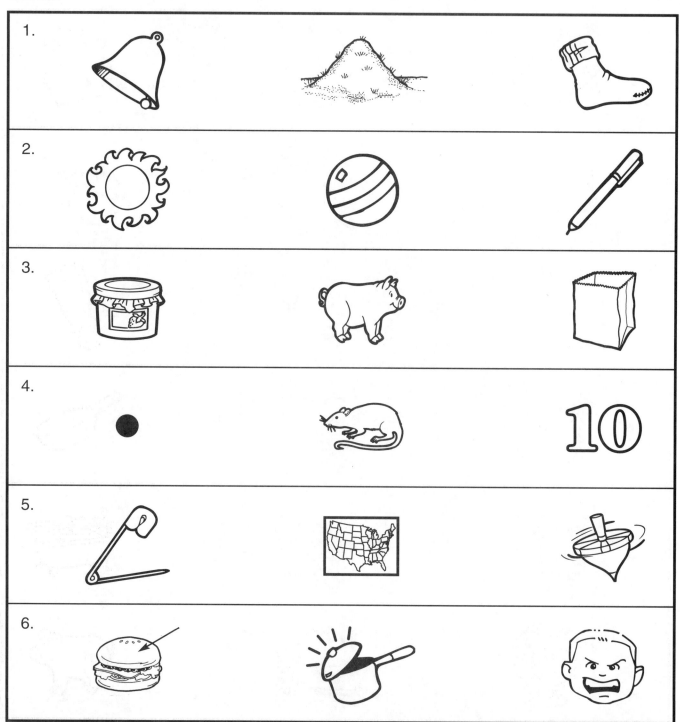

Doesn't Belong (cont.)

Medial Sounds

Directions: Look at the pictures in each row. Say each word. Cross off the word in each row that does not have the same middle sound as the other two words.

Phoneme Blending Activities

Phoneme blending requires students to combine a series of separate sounds in order to form a word. For example, students should be able to combine the sounds /t/, /o/, and /p/ in order to say the word *top*. Phoneme blending activities allow students to see how individual sounds make up words.

I Spy

Play I Spy with objects in the classroom as mystery words. Before saying the sounds of the word, provide a clue. For example, if the mystery word is *rug*, you might say, "I spy something in the room that is on the ground. It is blue. It is a /r/ . . . /u/ . . . /g/." Continue with other objects in the room. Challenge students to be the person who calls out the mystery I Spy word. The student providing the word will be practicing segmenting and the children guessing the word will be practicing blending.

Student Names

An excellent way to practice blending is with student names. Dismiss students from the carpet or to lunch by segmenting their names. The students have to blend the sounds to determine who is dismissed. For example, you may dismiss /j/ . . . /e/ . . . /s/. Once students are familiar with the blending activity, they will all guess Jess is the person being dismissed. Students always anxiously anticipate their names being segmented.

Four in a Row

Four in a Row provides blending practice for students. Six versions of student playing cards are provided on pages 32–34. Photocopy the playing cards on cardstock paper. Laminate for durability, if desired. Distribute the playing cards to students, one per child. Students will also need space markers such as buttons, small pieces of paper, or math manipulatives.

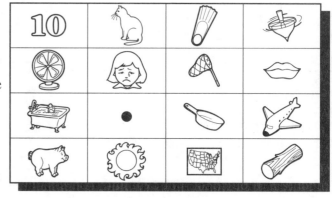

Photocopy and cut up the Segmented Word Cards on page 31 and place in a pile facedown. Select one card from the pile. Say the segmented sounds listed on the card. Students must blend the sounds together to determine the word. If the picture of the word is on their card, they can place a space marker on the picture. The first student to get four in a row across, down, or diagonally wins the game.

This game can also be adapted to practice phoneme isolation or phoneme identity. Use the same student playing cards, and simply adapt the way you present the word on the Segmented Word Card. For example, if you want to adapt the game to practice phoneme identity and the word on the Segmented Word Card is "/d/ /o/ /g/," simply change your direction. "You can put a marker on a space if you have a picture of a word beginning with the same sound as *dog*."

Segmented Word Cards

/c/ /a/ /t/	/p/ /a/ /n/	/f/ /i/ /n/	/t/ /o/ /p/
/f/ /a/ /n/	/s/ /a/ /d/	/n/ /e/ /t/	/l/ /i/ /p/
/t/ /u/ /b/	/d/ /o/ /t/	/r/ /a/ /n/	/j/ /e/ /t/
/p/ /i/ /g/	/m/ /a/ /p/	/s/ /u/ /n/	/l/ /o/ /g/
/t/ /e/ /n/	/c/ /a/ /n/	/h/ /a/ /n/ /d/	/p/ /o/ /t/
/n/ /e/ /s/ /t/	/p/ /i/ /n/	/w/ /i/ /g/	/m/ /o/ /p/
/b/ /u/ /g/	/h/ /a/ /t/	/v/ /a/ /n/	/r/ /i/ n/ /g/

Four-in-a-Row Playing Cards

Four-in-a-Row Playing Cards (cont.)

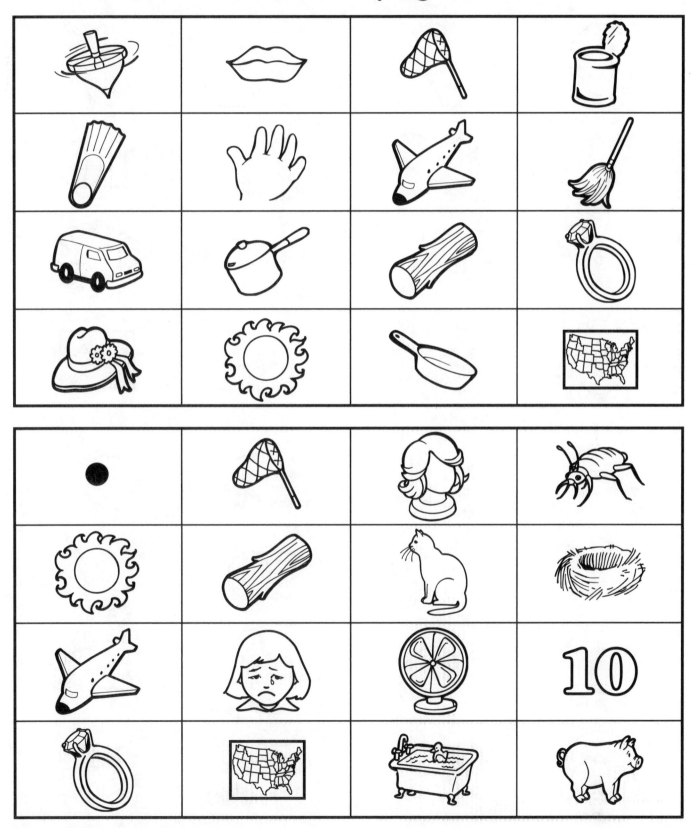

Four-in-a-Row Playing Cards (cont.)

Phoneme Segmentation Activities

Phoneme Segmentation activities provide students practice in isolating each sound in a word—beginning, medial, and ending. When segmenting a word, students must say each sound they hear in the word, one sound at a time. For example, if the word is *hat*, a student would say "/h/ . . . /a/ . . . /t/." Students can practice segmenting and blending activities with each other with one person doing the segmenting and the other person blending the segmented sounds.

Rhythm Instruments

Provide each student with a rhythm instrument. Tambourines, castanets, hand-held drums, and triangles can be used to indicate how many sounds there are in a word. Have the student shake or strike the instrument as he or she says each sound in the word. If you don't have rhythm instruments, have students use their bodies as instruments. Have students clap, snap, or jump in order to indicate the sounds in a word.

Animal Name Game

Use animal names for segmenting practice. Divide students into groups of two teams. Photocopy the animal picture cards on pages 24–26. Flip a coin to determine which team goes first. Show the first person one of the animal picture cards. If the student can successfully segment the word, his or her team receives one point. Then, the other team gets a chance to compete for a point. The team with the most points at the end of the game wins.

Sock Puppets

Have students make sock puppets from socks and various craft materials. Students can practice segmenting words by opening and closing their puppets' mouths for each sound in a word.

Egg Carton Game

Photocopy page 36 or 37 on cardstock paper. Determine if you will be using the pictures of CVC words (consonant–vowel–consonant words), words with initial blends, final blends, or digraphs. Cut out the circles and glue them to the inside of an egg carton, one circle per compartment. Have a student place a button inside the egg carton and close the lid. The student shakes the egg carton and then opens the lid again. He or she must look in which compartment the button landed, look at the picture and say the word, and then segment it. Students can play for fun or take turns with a partner and play for points. This activity is ideal to be placed in a literacy center once students have been introduced to how to use the egg carton. Also, the same egg carton and pictures can be used to practice isolating initial or ending sounds; or students can practice phoneme categorization by thinking of another word that begins with the same sound as the picture.

Egg-Carton Picture Circles

CVC Words

Words with Initial Blends

36

Egg-Carton Picture Circles (cont.)

Words with Ending Blends

Words with Digraphs

Phoneme Deletion Activities

In phoneme deletion activities, students delete a sound and say the remaining word. For example, if you delete the initial sound in the word *park*, you would get the word *ark*.

Phoneme Deletion

The words listed below are excellent for practicing phoneme deletion. After deleting the initial sound of these words, another real word remains.

boat → (oat)	can → (an)	face → (ace)
fin → (in)	hair → (air)	jar → (are)
mice → (ice)	pink → (ink)	sand → (and)
box → (ox)	cold → (old)	fall → (all)
game → (aim)	hand → (and)	late → (ate)
pan → (an)	rat → (at)	seal → (eel)
bus → (us)	dark → (ark)	fan → (an)
gate → (ate)	hat → (at)	lie → (I)
peel → (eel)	rice → (ice)	wade → (aid)
by → (I)	date → (ate)	feet → (eat)
goat → (oat)	hit → (it)	man → (an)
pie → (I)	sad → (add)	witch → (itch)

Nonsense Words

Words used in phoneme deletion activities can either yield real or nonsense words once the initial sound is deleted. For example, you could have students delete the initial sound from the word *dot*, yielding *ot*. Have students practice deleting initial sounds in which the remaining word is nonsense. This is an excellent assessment of students' understanding of phoneme deletion.

Words with Blends

A component of first grade is for students to learn about blends. Provided on page 39 is a list of words beginning with blends. When the initial sound from the blend is deleted, a real word remains. Ask students to delete the initial sound from these words in order to practice phoneme deletion, as well as blends.

Deleting Ending Sounds

Once students have a good understanding of how to delete initial sounds of words, challenge them to delete sounds in other positions. For example, ask students to delete the ending sound in the word *belt*. Students should indicate that the remaining word is *bel* (*bell*).

Blends for Phoneme Addition/Deletion

black → (lack)

blade → (laid)

bled → (led)

blend → (lend)

blink → (link)

block → (lock)

blow → (low)

brain → (rain)

brake → (rake)

bran → (ran)

break → (rake)

bright → (right)

bring → (ring)

claim → (lame)

clap → (lap)

clean → (lean)

cleft → (left)

climb → (lime)

clip → (lip)

clock → (lock)

clog → (log)

cloud → (loud)

crack → (rack)

cramp → (ramp)

crane → (rain)

crank → (rank)

crash → (rash)

crate → (rate)

crib → (rib)

crock → (rock)

crow → (row)

crumble → (rumble)

drag → (rag)

draw → (raw)

drift → (rift)

drink → (rink)

drug → (rug)

flame → (lame)

flash → (lash)

flap → (lap)

flock → (lock)

flow → (low)

flush → (lush)

fly → (lie)

frank → (rank)

flock → (lock)

gland → (land)

glide → (lied)

globe → (lobe)

grace → (race)

grade → (raid)

grain → (rain)

grate → (rate)

gray → (ray)

graze → (raise)

grid → (rid)

grip → (rip)

ground → (round)

place → (lace)

plain → (lain)

play → (lay)

player → (layer)

plight → (light)

plump → (lump)

plunge → (lunge)

prank → (rank)

pride → (ride)

prince → (rinse)

proof → (roof)

prose → (rose)

scan → (can)

scare → (care)

scold → (cold)

skid → (kid)

slash → (lash)

slip → (lip)

slam → (lamb)

slow → (low)

small → (mall)

smash → (mash)

snap → (nap)

space → (pace)

spade → (paid)

spare → (pare)

spark → (park)

speech → (peach)

spill → (pill)

spin → (pin)

spit → (pit)

spore → (pour)

spot → (pot)

spout → (pout)

stake → (take)

start → (tart)

stick → (tick)

stock → (tock)

stone → (tone)

stop → (top)

store → (tore)

swag → (wag)

swarm → (warm)

swash → (wash)

sway → (way)

sweep → (weep)

sweet → (wheat)

swing → (wing)

track → (rack)

twig → (wig)

Phoneme Addition Activities

Phoneme addition is the exact opposite of phoneme deletion. Students must add a sound in order to make a new word. For example, ask students, "What word will you get if you add /r/ to the beginning of the word *ate*?" Students should indicate *rate*. As in phoneme deletion, the new word created can be either a real word or a nonsense word.

Adding Onsets

Tell students that you want them to practice phoneme addition—for example, /d/. This sound will be the onset of the new words you will be making. Then, provide students a variety of rimes to which students will practice adding the onset. A list of suggested rimes is provided below. Have students add the sound to create new words. Use all of the rimes provided, even if the resulting word will be a nonsense word.

/ack/ → dack	/ar/ → dar	/ill/ → dill
/ad/ → dad	/at/ → dat	/it/ → dit
/ag/ → dag	/ay/ → day	/old/ → dold
/all/ → dall	/ed/ → ded	/ug/ → dug
/ake/ → dake	/est/ → dest	/un/ → dun
/and/ → dand	/ig/ → dig	/y/ → dy

Have students determine which words are real and which are nonsensical. Try adding a different initial sound to these rimes in order to create new words.

New Names

Have students add a sound to the beginning of their names. For example, if your class has been learning about the letter *T*, students can add the /t/ sound to the beginning of their names. The name *Ron* would become *Tron*. Students love to make these changes to their names. Have students use their new names for the day.

Making Blends

Have students practice phoneme addition in order to make new words with blends. See page 39 for a list of words that can be used to practice blends. For example, if the word is *crank*, you will need to delete the initial sound to make the word *rank*. Ask students, "What word do you get if you add /c/ to the beginning of the word *rank*?"

Phoneme Substitution Activities

By substituting one sound in a word for another, students are practicing phoneme substitution. For example, if you say the word *jet* and substitute /g/ for the /j/, the new word is *get*. As with phoneme addition and deletion activities, the new word created can be either a real word or a nonsense word.

Initial and Ending Sound Substitutions

Have students begin by practicing phoneme substitution with initial sounds. Once students become skilled at substituting initial sounds, have them practice substituting ending sounds.

Through the Alphabet

Create real and nonsense words by substituting the sounds of the alphabet combined with a rime. For example, if the rime is *-at*, have students substitute all the consonant sounds of the alphabet, as the initial sound to create new words:

bat	jat	quat	xat
cat	kat	rat	yat
dat	lat	sat	zat
fat	mat	tat	
gat	nat	vat	
hat	pat	wat	

Name Change

A fun way to practice phoneme substitution is with students' names. Substitute the initial sound in a student's name with a sound currently being studied. For example, if the class is learning about the letter B, have students practice substituting /b/ for the initial sound in their names. *John* would become *Bohn*. Students really have a great time with this activity and will often want to be called their new names for the entire day or longer.

Vowel Changes

Have the students practice making phoneme substitutions of medial vowels in CVC words. Begin by saying a CVC word. Students substitute each of the vowels (*a*, *e*, *i*, *o*, and *u*) in place of the medial vowel in order to create new words. For example, if you say the word *hat*, students would substitute the vowel to create the words *het, hit, hot,* and *hut*. Have students identify which of the new words are real words and which are nonsense words.

Phonics

Phonics instruction provides students an opportunity to develop their understanding of the relationship between letters and sounds. A good understanding of the relationships between letters and sounds is needed for students to be successful readers. Although our language does have many irregularly spelled words in which a straight letter/sound relationship (one sound for one letter) does not work, it is still a system that can be used to help decode words. Students can learn to read irregular words through a variety of other means such as spelling patterns and memory.

Your reading or phonics program probably prescribes a sequence for teaching phonics concepts. Use this section of the book as a supplement to your program. The purpose of this section is not to provide a systematic approach to teaching phonics, but rather to provide ideas of ways students can develop their understanding of the sound/symbol relationship. Use or adapt the ideas in this section to the phonics concepts on which you are currently working. As you work in this section, there are two important terms to know.

> *Onset*—the beginning sound/s of a word up to the vowel
>
> *Rime*—the vowel plus the remaining sounds in a word

For example, in the word crab, "cr" is the onset and "ab" is the rime.

✏ Initial and Ending Sounds

Practice identifying initial and ending sounds, including initial blends.

✏ Medial Sounds

Practice identifying and reading long and short vowel words, as well as manipulating vowel sounds.

✏ Word Families

Practice making and reading short-vowel word families.

Letter/Sound Assessment

Assessing a student's existing knowledge of letters and sounds will help you determine the areas in which the student needs instruction. One way to get a good picture of a student's knowledge of letters and sounds is to give him or her a Letter/Sound Assessment. This assessment is given one-on-one. In the assessment, students are asked to name each uppercase and lowercase letter of the alphabet and produce the corresponding sound. By recording the results on a data sheet, you are able to easily see how a student scored, which will help you in determining areas on which to focus.

Photocopy one copy of the upper- and lowercase letters on pages 44 and 45. Make one photocopy per student of the Student Data Sheet on page 46. Begin with the uppercase letters. Show the student the photocopy of the uppercase letters (page 44), one row at a time. First, ask the student to name each letter. Mark an **X** in the corresponding box on the student data sheet to indicate the letters the student has correctly identified. Then, ask the student to produce the corresponding sound. Again, mark an **X** in the corresponding box on the student data sheet.

Continue the assessment by showing the student the photocopy of the lowercase letters (page 45). Once again, mark an **X** in the corresponding box on the student data sheet to indicate the letters and sounds the student has correctly identified. Use the student data sheet to determine which lessons and readers you will use from the book.

Uppercase Letters

1. T Q V U X

2. M Z B I F

3. Y O K P D

4. E G L H A

5. R W S C J

6. N

Lowercase Letters

1. t q v u x

2. m z b i f

3. y o k p d

4. e g l h a

5. r w s c j

6. n

Student Data Sheet

Student's Name: _____   Date: _____

Uppercase Letters	Identifies Letter	Produces Sound
T		
Q		
V		
U		
X		
M		
Z		
B		
I		
F		
Y		
O		
K		
P		
D		
E		
G		
L		
H		
A		
R		
W		
S		
C		
J		
N		
Totals	**/26**	**/26**

Lowercase Letters	Identifies Letter	Produces Sound
t		
q		
v		
u		
x		
m		
z		
b		
i		
f		
y		
o		
k		
p		
d		
e		
g		
l		
h		
a		
r		
w		
s		
c		
j		
n		
Totals	**/26**	**/26**

Phonics Activities

Decorate a Letter

Provide a cut-out of the letter that you are currently studying. Gather materials that begin with that letter, which the students can glue onto the letter cut-out. For example, students can glue buttons on the letter *B* or cotton balls on the letter *C*.

Magazine Search

Collect old magazines and ask students to look for and cut out pictures that begin or end with the sound on which you are currently working. For example, if you are focusing on the letter *G*, students should search for pictures or words that begin with the letter *G*. Students can glue their pictures on a piece of chart paper or a large sheet of construction paper. If you do this activity for each letter of the alphabet, the pages can be assembled into a class alphabet book.

Hopscotch

Draw a hopscotch on the ground outside your classroom. Label the boxes with letters instead of numbers. Students play hopscotch with normal rules, except they must name each letter as they jump in the squares. Adapt the game as needed to have students say the sound the letter makes or think of a word that begins with that letter.

Sound Containers

Create sound containers. Save plastic containers such as margarine tubs. Label each container with a letter of the alphabet. Begin searching your house and classroom for small objects to put in each container. The objects go into the letter container that corresponds to the first sound (or last if you prefer) of the object. Try to find at least five objects for each container. Then, when you are introducing a letter and its sound to students, you will have a container of objects that begin with that letter and sound to illustrate your point. You may even choose to create a container for blends. Be on a constant lookout for new objects to place in your containers.

Use the sound containers as a game or assessment by taking objects out of the containers and asking students to place the objects back into the correct containers.

Heads or Tails

Determine a letter that you want students to practice—for example, *N*. Then, have a student flip a coin. If the coin lands on the heads side, the student must think of a word that begins with *N*. If the coin lands on the tails side, the student must think of a word that ends with *N*.

Phonics Activities (cont.)

Go Fish

Create a pond by shaping a piece of blue yarn into a circle on the floor. Make a fishing rod (see the directions below). Gather magnetic letters and place them in the pond. Select a student to go first. The student must use the fishing rod to catch a letter. (The magnet on the end of the fishing rod attracts a magnetic letter.) The student must then identify the letter and name a word that begins with the same sound the letter makes. If the student correctly identifies a word beginning with that letter, he or she gets to keep the letter. Then tell the second student to go fish. The student with the most letters at the end of the round wins the game.

Challenge students who are ready to think of words that end with the letter that is drawn.

How to Make a Fishing Rod

Gather ½" dowel rod, 18" (46 cm) in length; string; and a magnet. Staple a piece of string that is about 2' (61 cm) long to one of the ends of a dowel. Tie the magnet to the end of the string.

Variations on Go Fish

➤ Photocopy page 32 onto cardstock. Cut out the picture cards Tape a paperclip to the back of each card. Place the cards in the pond. Students must fish for a card and then spell the word. Provide small whiteboards and markers or a piece of paper and pencils on which the students can write the words.

➤ Photocopy page 32 onto cardstock. Cut out the picture cards. Tape a paperclip to the back of each card. Place the cards in the pond. Students go fishing for the word cards. Have students think of a word that rhymes with the card drawn.

➤ Photocopy page 32 onto cardstock. Cut out the picture cards. Tape a paperclip to the back of each card. Place the cards in the pond. Students go fishing for the word cards. Have students think of a word that begins with the same sound as the picture on the card. An alternative is for students to think of a word that ends with the same sound as the picture on the card.

➤ Photocopy page 83. Stack the rime cards facedown. For each round, the teacher draws a rime card and students fish for a letter. If the letter makes a word with the rime the student gets one point. The student with the most points at the end of the game wins. For example, the teacher may turn over the rime card *–ed*. The first student goes fishing and draws the letter *b*. The word *bed* can be made, and the student would be awarded one point. If the second student goes fishing and draws the letter *c*, the word *ced* is not a word, and no point would be awarded. Draw a new rime card at the beginning of each round.

Phonics Activities (cont.)

Grocery Store

Photocopy the circles below and the art on page 50, one for each child. Cut out the letter circles at the bottom of this page. Have the students color the pictures on page 50. Then have them name each item in the grocery store and match the letter to the picture that begins with that letter. They can glue the letter circle above or on each picture. You can extend the activity by asking students to identify the ending sound of each word. Write the ending letter above the picture.

Consider making this activity into a file-folder game. Make copies of page 50. Color and glue them on the insides of file folders. Staple an envelope or self-sealing baggie to the back of each file folder. Cut out the letters at the bottom of this page and store in the baggie. Another suggestion is to gather the corresponding magnetic alphabet letters and have students match those letters by placing them on top of the pictures. This activity is ideal for a literacy center.

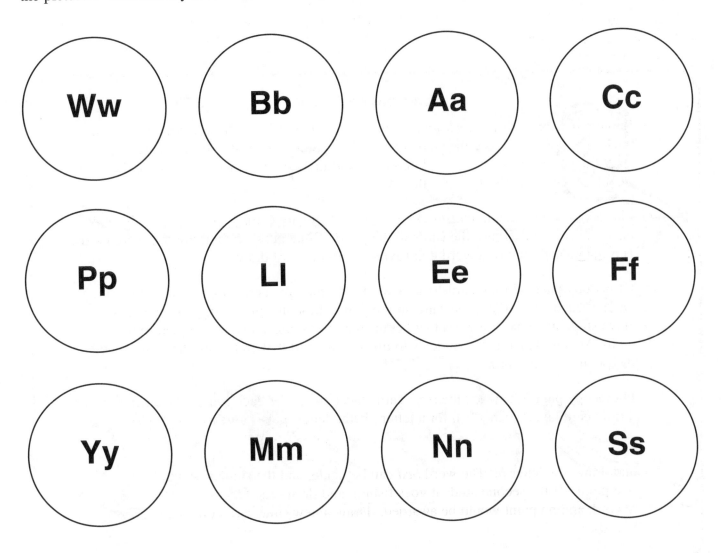

Grocery Store (cont.)

Phonics Activities (cont.)

Toy Shop

Photocopy the art below and on page 52, one for each child. Cut out the letter circles at the bottom of this page. Have the students color the pictures on page 52. Then have them name each item in the toy shop and match the letter to the picture that begins with that letter. They can glue the letter circle above or on each picture. You can extend the activity by asking students to identify the ending sound of each word. Write the ending letter above the picture.

Consider making this activity into a file folder game. Make copies of page 52. Color and glue them on the insides of file folders. Staple an envelope or self-sealing baggie to the back of each file folder. Cut out the letters at the bottom of this page and store in the baggie. Another suggestion is to gather the corresponding magnetic alphabet letters and have students match those letters by placing them on top of the pictures. This activity is ideal for a literacy center.

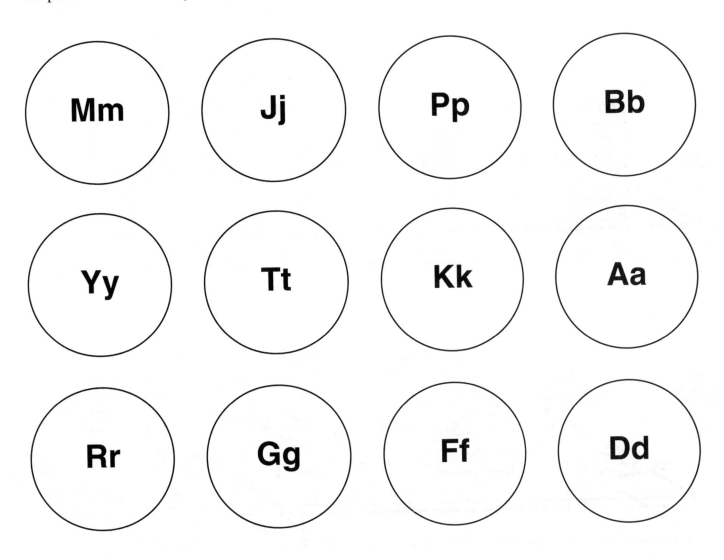

Toy Shop (cont.)

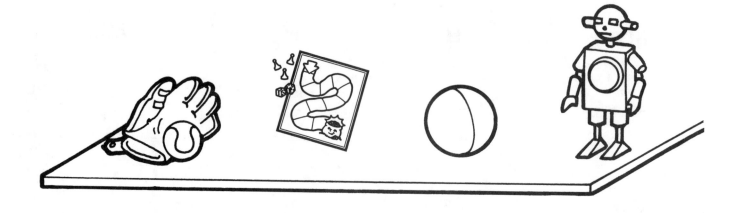

52

Initial Sounds

Directions: Cut out the picture cards at the bottom of the page. Glue each card in the correct column. Write the word.

Begins with Dd	Begins with Jj	Begins with Qq

Initial Sounds (cont.)

Directions: Look at the pictures. Say each word. Write the beginning letter on the line to complete the words.

1. 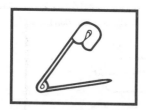 _____ an

7. 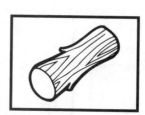 _____ og

2.  _____ an

8.  _____ og

3.  _____ un

9.  _____ en

4.  _____ un

10.  _____ en

5.  _____ in

11.  _____ at

6.  _____ in

12.  _____ at

Ending Sounds

Directions: Cut out the picture cards at the bottom of the page. Glue each card in the correct column. Write the word.

Ends with Nn	**Ends with Pp**	**Ends with Tt**

Ending Sounds (cont.)

Directions: Look at the pictures. Say each word. Write the ending letter on the line to complete the words.

1.  _____
do

2.  _____
do

3. 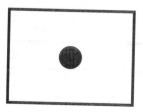 _____
tu

4.  _____
tu

5.  _____
pi

6.  _____
pi

7.  _____
ha

8.  _____
ha

9.  _____
ca

10.  _____
ca

11.  _____
su

12. 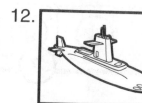 _____
su

Egg-Carton Games

Create egg-carton games that can be used as whole-class, small-group, or partner phonics activities. Corresponding pieces to assemble these games can be found on pages 58 and 59. Use the directions below or alter them to best meet the needs of your students. Consider placing the egg-carton games in a literacy center once you have taught students how to play them.

Think of a Word

Cut out the blend circles on page 58. Pictures of 20 blends are provided. Use the 12 pictures that are most appropriate to those you have been studying. Glue the circles to the inside bottom of an egg carton, one circle per compartment. Provide a button to go with the game. Students are to place the button inside the egg carton, close the lid, and shake the carton. Then, they open the lid and look in which compartment the button landed. Students must think of a word that begins with the blend that is in the same compartment as the button. Close the lid and repeat.

Name the Blend

Cut out the picture circles on page 59. Twenty blends are provided. Use the 12 blends that are most appropriate to those you have been studying. Glue the pictures to the inside bottom of an egg carton, one picture per compartment. Provide a button to go with the game. Students are to place the button inside the egg carton, close the lid, and shake the carton. Then, they open the lid and look in which compartment the button landed. Students must look at the picture and say the word. They must then identify the blend at the beginning of the word.

An alternative to this activity is to have students name the medial or ending letter that corresponds to the picture. Have students who are ready, spell the words.

Match the Blend

Cut out both the picture circles and blend circles on pages 58 and 59. Glue the picture circles to the inside bottoms of two egg cartons, one picture per compartment. Name each picture. Students must match the blends by placing a letter circle in the compartments with the picture that begins with the blend.

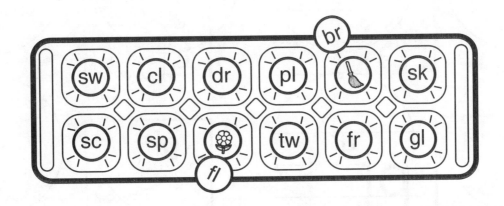

Blend Circles

fl	fr	pl	pr
tr	sp	sw	sk
sl	tw	sn	sm
sc	dr	cl	bl
br	gr	gl	cr

Picture Circles

Match the Blends

Directions: Cut out the picture cards at the bottom of the page. Say each word. Glue the picture cards in the box with the letters for the initial blend.

cr	dr
fr	**gr**

Butterfly Blends

Directions: Cut out the picture circles below. Say each word. Sort the pictures by initial blend. Glue the picture circles on the correct wings of the butterfly.

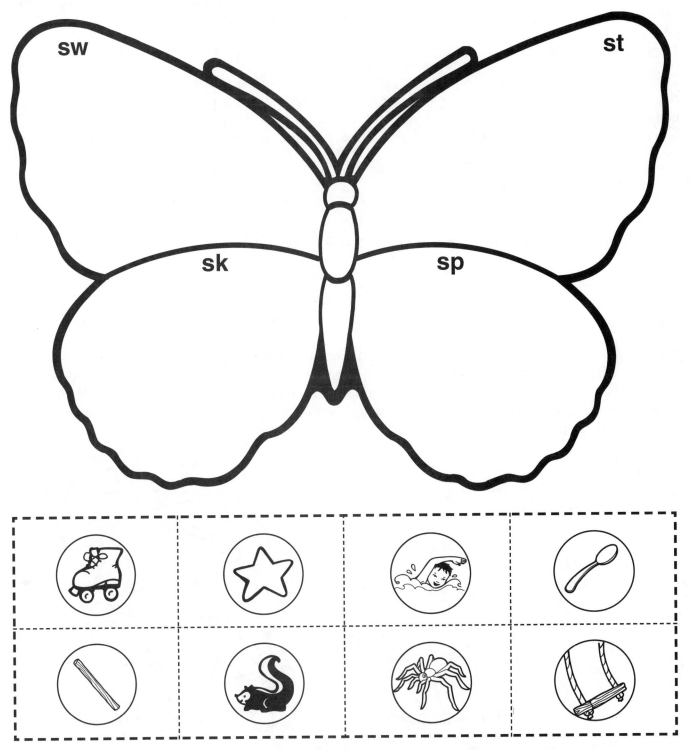

Medial Sounds Activities

Long or Short?

Have students stand. Tell students you are going to say a word. If the word has a short vowel sound, they should squat down to be very short. If the word has a long vowel sound, students should stand up tall. Provide a variety of long and short vowel words for students to practice.

Makes Many Words

Demonstrate for students the effects of changing the vowel in words. Write the letters in the words below on index cards, one letter per index card. Display the letters in a pocket chart. Have volunteers come to the pocket chart to make the words with the index cards. Try each of the vowels as medial letters to see if a word is formed. Change the vowels to create new words or nonsense words.

Letters: h, t, b, g, p, f, n, a, e, i, o, u

Example:	h_t	hat	het	hit	hot	hut
	b_g	bag	beg	big	bog	bug
	f_n	fan	fen	fin	fon	fun
	p_n	pan	pen	pin	pon	pun

From Short to Long

Demonstrate the effects of changing a short vowel sound to a long vowel sound. Write the short vowel words on index cards. Write the letter *e* on another index card. Have students read the short vowel word. Then, add the *e* to the end of the word and have the students read the long vowel words. Students can fold a piece of paper into boxes, write several pairs of words, and draw a picture to correspond to each word.

Example:

cap → cape   van → vane

kit → kite   hat → hate

tap → tape   mat → mate

rip → ripe   fin → fine

bit → bite   pin → pine

tub → tube   sit → site

can → cane   hop → hope

man → mane   fad → fade

mad → made

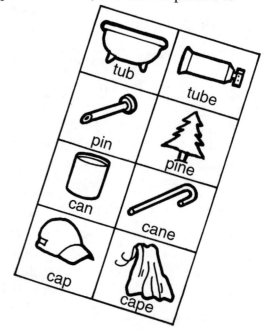

Medial Sounds Activities

Vowel Sort

Pages 64–68 provide picture/word cards for each of the vowels. Although the activity below is described with the vowel *A*, the same activity can made for each of the vowels.

Photocopy page 64 onto cardstock paper. Color and cut out the pieces. Laminate for durability, if desired. Glue the "Short Aa" label to one brown paper bag and the "Long Aa" label to another brown paper bag. Have students look at the pictures on each card and read each word. If the word has a short *a* sound (as in *ant*), students should place the picture card in the "Short Aa" bag. If the word has a long *a* sound (as in *ape*), students should place the picture card in the "Long Aa" bag. If desired, you can color code the back of the picture/word cards so students can self-check. For example, color a small red dot on the back of the "Short Aa" picture/word cards and a small blue dot on the back of the "Long Aa" picture/word cards. Once introduced, this activity makes a great learning-center activity.

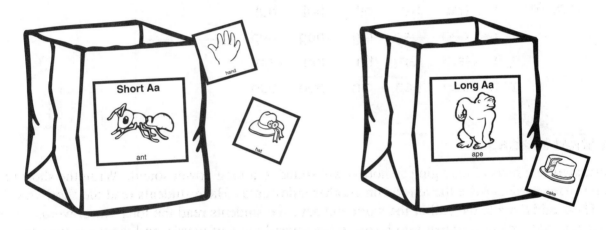

Vowel Concentration

Photocopy the vowel picture/word cards on pages 64–68. Color and cut out. Laminate for durability, if desired. Two to four players can play this game at a time. Place all of the picture/word cards facedown on the floor or table. The first player begins by turning over two cards. He or she looks at the pictures and reads the word on the cards. If the words both have the same vowel sound, he or she may keep the pair. If the words do not have the same vowel sound, he or she must turn the cards back over. If a match is made, the student gets to take another turn. Play continues as students take turns turning over two cards at a time. Students must concentrate in order to remember where potential matches are located. Students continue to turn over two cards at a time until all of the pairs have been picked up. The player with the most pairs wins the game.

The words do not necessarily have to have the same spelling pattern, just the same vowel sound. For example, if a player turns over the words *suit* and *flute*, the pair matches because both words have a long *u* sound. Also, teach students to play the game even if you have not introduced all the long and short vowels. For example, students can still play the game using only the long and short *a* and *e* cards.

Vowel Cards (A)

Short Aa	**Long Aa**
ant	ape
hat	map	rake	gate
bag	can	rain	cake
hand	sad	game	hay

Vowel Cards (E)

Short Ee	Long Ee
egg	eagle
bed	bell	seed	ear
nest	pen	seal	feet
ten	net	leaf	peach

Vowel Cards (I)

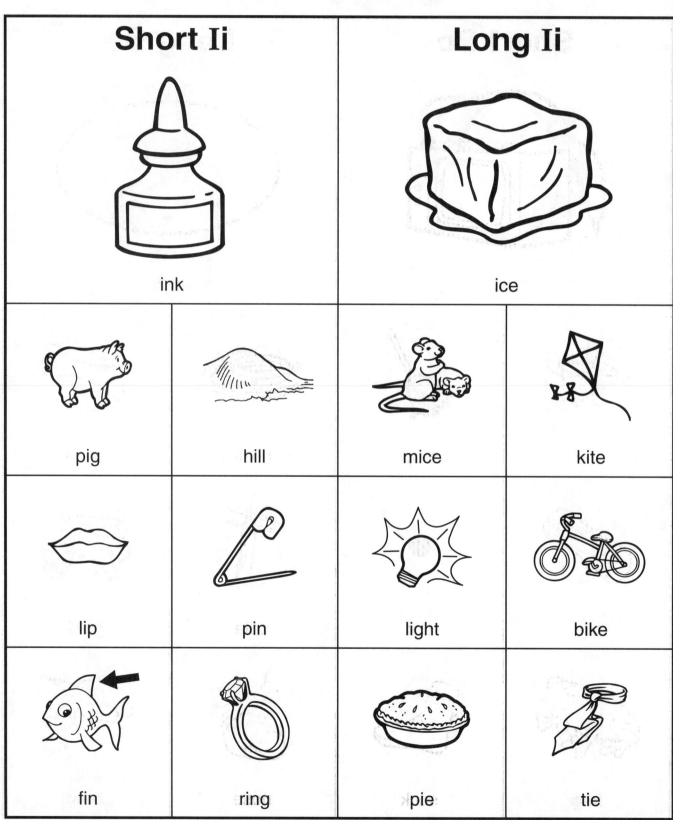

Short Ii	**Long Ii**
ink	ice
pig	hill	mice	kite
lip	pin	light	bike
fin	ring	pie	tie

Vowel Cards (O)

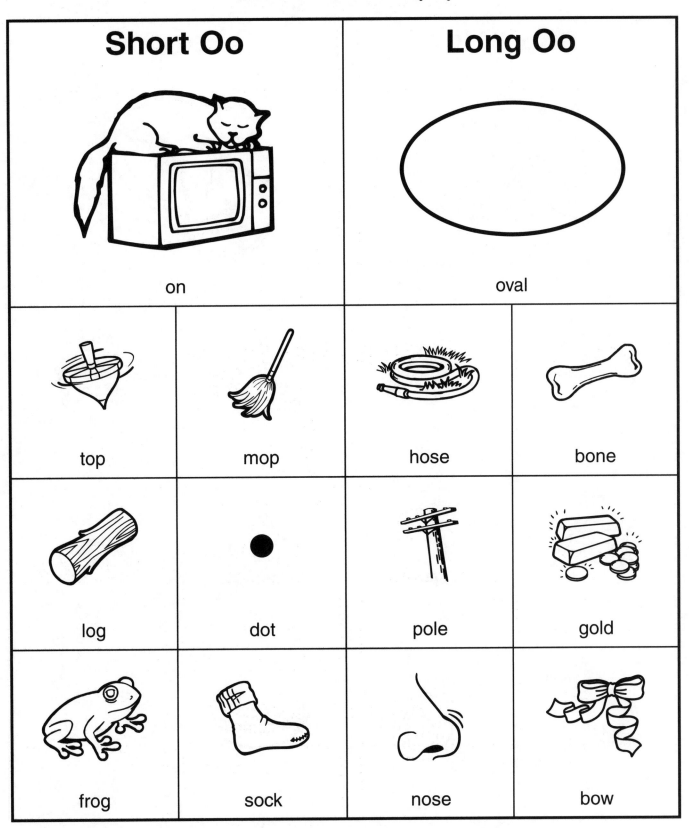

Short Oo	Long Oo
on	oval
top	hose
mop	bone
log	pole
dot	gold
frog	nose
sock	bow

Vowel Cards (U)

Short Uu	Long Uu
umbrella	ukulele

tub	rug	suit	mule

bug	sun	juice	fruit

nut	hug	flute	cube

More Medial Sounds Activities

Sing Vowel Words

Compose words to the tune of familiar children's songs in order to reinforce long and short vowel sounds. The tune below—"Have You Heard Some Short *e* Words'—can be adapted to any long or short vowel sound. Simply change the words to the song to reinforce the vowel sound you want students to practice. Once students become familiar with the tune and how the words of the song work, have students take on the role of the teacher and determine words that have the target vowel sound. For example, the teacher can provide the name of the song, "Have You Heard Some Long *i* Words?" Select a student to sing the teacher lines of the song, including determining the long *i* words that are at the end of the verse. The remaining students can reply with the student verse.

"Have You Heard Some Short *e* Words?"
(to the tune of "Do You Know the Muffin Man?")

Teacher: Do you know some short *e* words, some short *e* words, some short *e* words?

Do you know some short *e* words, like *let* and *nest* and *egg*?

Students: Yes, we know some short *e* words, some short *e* words, some short *e* words.

Yes, we know some short *e* words, like *let* and *nest* and *egg*.

Roll for a Vowel

Photocopy the die pattern on page 70 onto cardstock paper. Follow the directions in order to assemble the die. Determine which student will roll first. Once the die has stopped rolling, the student must look at what vowel is showing on top of the die. The student must then say a word with that vowel as the medial sound. If the student correctly says a word, he or she gets one point. If the student cannot determine a word or the word does not contain the correct vowel sound, he or she does not get a point. If the "Name the Vowel" side of the pattern is showing, the student may name any word and then name the vowel sound they hear in the word. Students take turns rolling the die and naming words. The student with 10 points first is the winner. This game may be adapted depending on whether you are working on long or short vowel sounds. For example, you may teach this game early in the year and have students say short vowel words. Later in the school year, you may require students to say long vowel words. Once students learn how to play this game, it makes an excellent learning center activity.

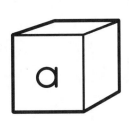 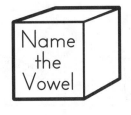 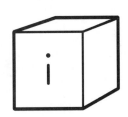

Die Pattern

Directions: Photocopy this page onto cardstock paper. Cut out the pattern on the solid lines. Fold the pattern on the dotted lines. Pull the pattern together in the shape of a cube. Place a small amount of glue on each of the tabs and tuck them inside the pattern. Allow to dry completely.

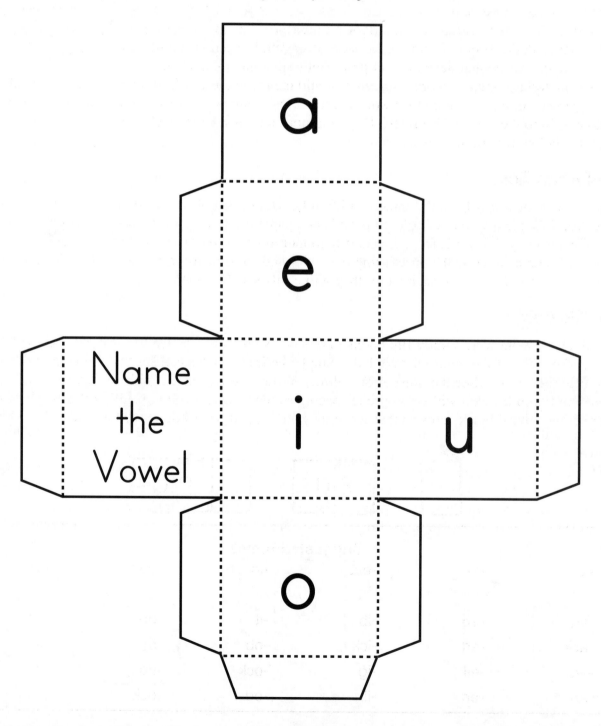

Word Families Activities

Word Family Clips

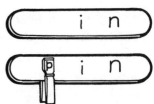

Write the letters A—Z, one each, on the tips of clothespins. These letters will become the onset (the beginning sound/s of a word up to the vowel) when forming new words. Write rimes (the vowel plus the remaining sounds in a word), one each on tongue depressors. Be sure to leave space for the clothespins. (See the illustration to the right.) Place the clothespins in one pile and the tongue depressors in another pile. Students should select one clothespin and one tongue depressor. Have them clip the clothespin onto the tongue depressor in order to make a word. Students should then read the word. If a real word is formed, the student gets one point. If a nonsense word is formed, no point is awarded. Return the tongue depressor and clothespin to their respective piles. Play continues until a student reaches a predetermined score. See the list below for common word families.

Colorful Families

Display a chart of words from the same word family. Draw a simple illustration to correspond with each word. Provide a variety of colored pencils and paper or dry eraser markers and whiteboards. Have students copy the words from the chart onto their own piece of paper or small whiteboard. Encourage students to copy the onset using one color and the rime using another color. If students keep the same color for the rime in each word, they will easily see the pattern.

Rime Flip Books

Have students create word-family flip books to practice word families. Gather five index cards for each student. Fold four of the index cards in half. Staple the folded index cards to the left side of the remaining index card. (See the illustration below.) Write an onset on the folded index card and the rime on the flat index card with appropriate spacing so they create a word. Continue writing onsets on the remaining folded index cards so that when they are flipped open a new word is revealed.

Suggested Rimes					
-ab	-ap	-est	-ip	-og	-ud
-ad	-at	-et	-ing	-old	-ug
-ag	-eb	-ib	-it	-op	-um
-ack	-ed	-ick	-ob	-ot	-un
-am	-ell	-ig	-ock	-ub	-ut
-an	-en	-ill	-od	-uck	

Word Families Activities (cont.)

Family Houses

Cut an outline of a house with a chimney out of construction paper. Label the chimney with a word family. Have students brainstorm words that will fit into the word family. For example, if the word family you are working on is -*et*, students may brainstorm the following words: *bet, get, jet, let, met, net, pet, set,* and *vet.* Encourage students to include words with blends that fit into the word family. You may also want students to include other words that have the word family in the spelling, but do not necessarily end with the word family. For example, in the -*et* word family, students may suggest a word such as *settle.*
You may want to include nonsense words students think of that contain the word family. For example, nonsense words for -*et* would be *det, cet, fet,* or *ret.* Make an asterisk next to the nonsense words in order to denote them as words that we do not use in our language. Keep the word-family houses on display in the classroom. Encourage students to add to the house lists throughout the year.

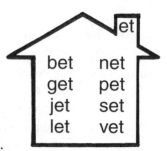

Word Family Circles

Photocopy page 73 onto cardstock, one for each student. Have students cut out both of the patterns on the page. Assemble together placing the whole circle on the bottom and the circle with the cut-out on the top. Secure together with a brad at the **X**. Have students label the top circle with a word family (for example, -*ug*). Then, have students spin the bottom wheel in order to write an initial consonant or blend that will make a word with the word family chunk. Students can practice spinning the wheel and reading the word family words.

Through the Alphabet

Create real and nonsense words by combining each of the sounds of the alphabet with a word family. For example, if the rime is -*et*, have students substitute all the consonant sounds as the initial sound to create new words (see below). Have students identify which words are real and which words are nonsense.

bet	fet	jet	met	quet	tet	xet
cet	get	ket	net	ret	vet	yet
det	het	let	pet	set	wet	zet

Word Family Circles

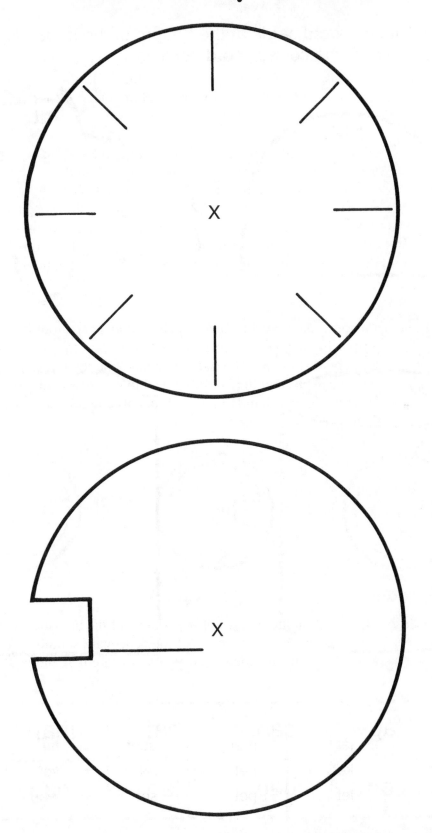

Short Aa Word Families

Directions: Cut out the word cards at the bottom of the page. Read the words. Glue the words to match the correct word families.

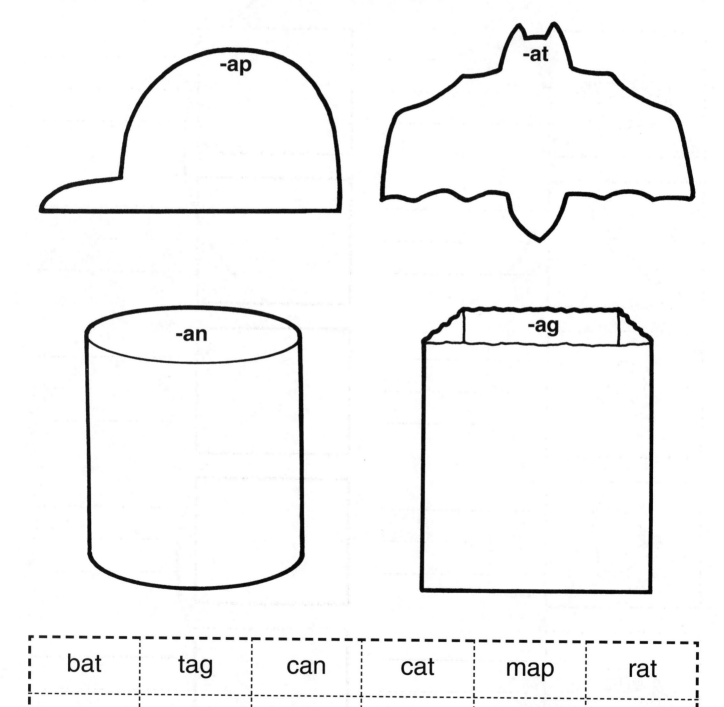

bat	tag	can	cat	map	rat
fan	cap	bag	tap	wag	man

Short Ee Word Families

Directions: Look at the pictures. Write the words. To the right, write another word that is in the same word family. Draw a picture to match the word.

Short Ii Word Families

Directions: Look at the pictures. Write two more words in the same word family. Draw a picture to match each word.

-ig

pig

-in

fin

-ip

tip

-it

hit

Short Oo Word Families

Directions: Look at the pictures in each row. Draw an **X** on the word that does not belong to the same word family as the other two words.

1.	dog	hog	hop
2.	mop	hot	top
3.	dot	pot	lock
4.	sock	jog	rock
5.	log	pop	jog
6.	cot	log	frog

Short Uu Word Families

Directions: Cut out the picture cards at the bottom of the page. Glue the picture cards in a row with the same word family. Write each word.

-un

-ug

-ub

Make a Word Game

Cut out the letter cards at the bottom of this page. Photocopy the game board on pages 80–81. Glue pages 80 and 81 to the inside of a file folder. Color and laminate, if desired. Staple an envelope or self-sealing baggie to the back of the file folder in which to store the letters. Cut out the game title and directions below and glue them to the front of the file folder. Gather objects that can be used as markers such as buttons or math counting cubes.

Demonstrate how to play the game for students. Then, allow students to play the game in pairs or triads. This is an excellent literacy-center activity.

Make a Word Game

Directions

Each player should select a marker. Place the letter cards in a pile facedown. Roll the die to determine who plays first. The first person rolls the die and moves the number indicated. Select the top letter card from the pile. Match the letter to the rime on the space. If a real word is formed, the player can roll again. If the word is a nonsense word, the player loses his or her turn. The player must remain on that space until he or she draws a letter that makes a real word.

Letter Cards				a
b	c	d	e	f
g	h	i	j	k
l	m	n	o	p
q	r	s	t	u
v	w	x	y	z

Game Board

Start	-ab	-ig	-ed	-ug

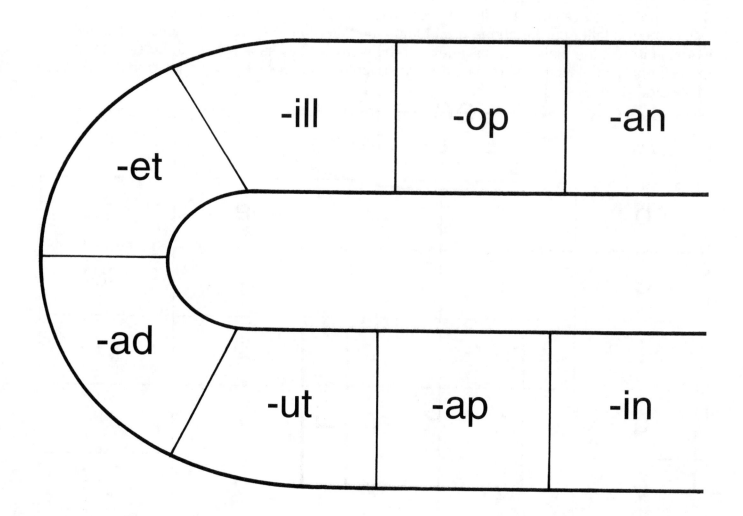

Game Board (cont.)

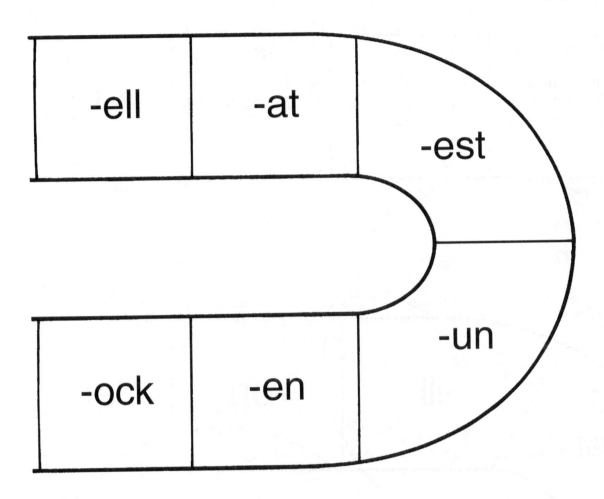

Spin a Word

In this game, students create words by spinning the first circle for the initial letter and the second circle for the rime. Students get one point for each time they spin and make a real word. No points are awarded for nonsense words. The player with the most points wins.

Directions: Photocopy this page onto cardstock and laminate for durability, if desired. Place a paperclip on the **X** in the center of the circle. Place the tip of a pencil inside the paperclip. Hold the pencil in place and spin the paperclip.

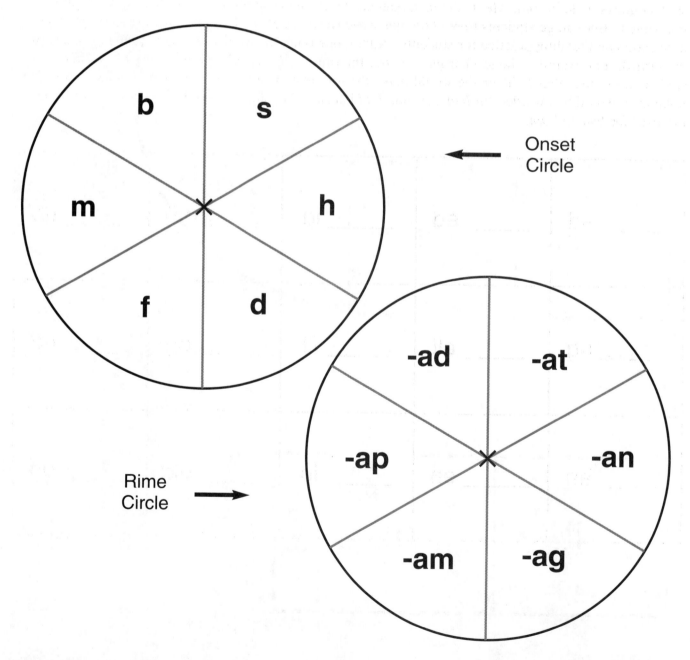

Clip a Word

Photocopy the cards below and on page 84 onto cardstock. Cut out the rime cards and laminate, if desired. Gather clothespins. Write the letters A–Z (and blends if appropriate) on the tips of clothespins. Place the clothespins in a pile and the rime cards in another pile. Students must draw a clothespin and a rime card. Have students clip the clothespin on the rime card to form a word. If a real word is formed, the student scores one point. Then the second child can draw a clothespin and rime card to try to make a word. The student with the most points at the end of the game, wins.

A variation is for the teacher to select five rime cards that every student will use on each turn. Each student draws a clothespin. He or she then matches up the letter to all five rime cards to try to make real words. Encourage students to read the nonsense words as well. This provides excellent phonics application and reading practice for students. Again, one point is awarded for each real word that can be formed. For example, the teacher may choose the rimes *-ed, -ig, -ub, -ot,* and *-ad.* If the first student draws the letter *b*, he or she would make the following words: *bed, big, bub, bot,* and *bad.* One point each would be awarded for *bed, big,* and *bad* because they are real words. No points would be awarded for *bub* and *bot.*

_____ ad	_____ ed	_____ ig	_____ ock	_____ ub
_____ ag	_____ ell	_____ ill	_____ og	_____ ud
_____ an	_____ en	_____ in	_____ old	_____ ug

Clip a Word (cont.)

_____ ap	_____ est	_____ ip	_____ op	_____ un
_____ at	_____ et	_____ it	_____ ot	_____ ut
_____ ace	_____ eat	_____ ice	_____ oat	_____ ube
_____ ake	_____ eet	_____ ike	_____ oke	_____ use
_____ ate	_____ eep	_____ ite	_____ ose	_____ ute

Fluency

Students who are fluent are able to recognize and read words quickly and accurately. Additionally, fluent readers have the ability to group words of text into meaningful sections. Fluent reading sounds much like natural speech. It is important to note that fluency is not merely the speed with which a passage is read. Fluent reading does have speed, yet there is also expression and there are pauses in the appropriate places at the text.

Fluency instruction cannot be understated. Fluency plays an important role in students' abilities to decode the words of a text and their abilities to understand the words of the text. If students can read fluently, they can focus on comprehension rather than reading the words.

There are many ways to promote fluency with beginning readers. Modeling fluent reading serves as an important component in reading instruction. When students observe the teacher or a parent reading to them, they are observing many aspects of a good reader. As a teacher or parent reads with expression, groups words into appropriate phrases, and reads naturally, rather than in choppy bits and pieces, students are immersed in what good reading sounds like. Additionally, students tend to emulate what is modeled for them. It is not unusual to see a child holding a book as if she or he was the teacher, reading a patterned or predictable book in a natural manner. Provided in this section are ideas for promoting read-alouds in the classroom.

Repeated readings of a text help students gain fluency, too. Finding authentic and fun ways for students to practice reading the same text over and over again provide for great gains in fluency. Reading books within a similar series, as well as learning and reciting poetry and songs, helps students develop reading fluency. By reciting poetry and singing songs, students begin to develop an understanding of the natural rhythm and flow of language. Ideas for promoting poetry and singing in the classroom are provided within this section.

At an appropriate level for beginning readers, other fluency instruction techniques such as choral reading, echo reading, tape-assisted reading, and partner reading help students make connections to concepts of print and develop fluency for predictable and patterned text they are able to read. Readers Theater is a technique that can also be used to promote rereading a text multiple times. Students love to prepare for a show and will undoubtedly be motivated to read and reread a script in order to get ready for a presentation. Sample Readers Theater scripts, as well as ideas for how to create your own Readers Theater scripts are included toward the end of this section.

Finally, students are motivated to read and reread a text when it is their own text they are reading. Provided within this section are samples of books that students can make and then practice reading and rereading. Fluency instruction, even with beginning readers, sets the stage for reading instruction that will come later in their schooling years.

Read-Alouds

Most teachers are already familiar with the benefits of reading to their classes; however, the benefits are so far reaching that they bear repeating. Reading out loud to students is an excellent opportunity to model reading with fluency to students. By listening to stories, plays, poems, and nonfiction texts, students are shown what good readers do when they read, as well as what good readers sound like. Reading aloud models fluent reading with appropriate phrasing, intonation, accuracy, and speed.

When teachers read aloud, they are modeling the natural flow and sound of written language. By reading with expression, emphasizing certain words, and pausing in the correct places students are shown that reading is more than just reading the words. Most teachers have a read-aloud time as part of their classroom schedule. Expand the types of text you read to your students by considering some of the examples below.

- ➤ fiction books
- ➤ nonfiction books
- ➤ magazine articles
- ➤ newspaper articles
- ➤ poetry
- ➤ cartoon strips
- ➤ notices and notes

- ➤ school bulletins
- ➤ letters
- ➤ song lyrics
- ➤ riddles
- ➤ jokes
- ➤ quotations

Although modeling reading a variety of texts is important, the reality is that books and poetry will provide the bulk of what we read to our students. Teachers can engage students by selecting quality books.

The Rule of Five

Some teachers use the Rule of Five when doing read-alouds in their classroom. The Rule of Five reminds teachers that students should be read aloud to five times each day. Although that may sound like a lot of time spent reading, remember the benefits of reading aloud to young children. The five read-alouds do not have to all be books. Incorporating poetry or other types of text into your day can reinforce topics on which your class is working, as well as provide a different genre with which students may not be familiar.

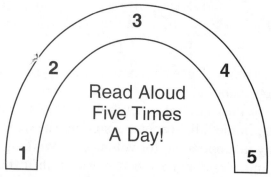

Read-Aloud Activities

Robot Reading

Demonstrate the importance of reading fluently by reading in a monotone voice. One day during your read-aloud time, read to students in a robot voice or monotone voice. You may also wish to read the words in a very choppy manner, not grouped into phrases as we normally read. Do not feel as though you have to read the whole story in this manner. Usually after a few sentences or paragraphs, students will have a strange look on their faces. Ask them what is wrong. Elicit from students that the reading was boring because it was read in one tone of voice, there was no expression, and the sentences ran together. Use this as a teaching opportunity to let students know that good readers read with fluency to make it easier to understand what is happening in the text.

Guest Reader

Having a guest reader is an excellent way of involving the school community or local community in classroom events. Some schools have a special day set aside in which they invite local community members to come into the classroom to read. You may want to organize this for your school or simply invite a community member to your room on a particular day. School-wide read-aloud days are especially fun to have when tied to an author's birthday (such as Dr. Seuss' birthday, which many schools are now celebrating).

Another idea is to invite various staff members to be special guest readers. On a regular basis, invite the principal, secretary, custodian, lunch supervisors, etc., into the classroom to read. Staff members who do not spend much time in the classroom love to come be the guest reader, and students love to see the various staff members in the classroom. Be sure to offer guest readers a book to preview or ask them if they would like to bring their favorite children's book from home.

Invite parents to come to your classroom as guest readers as well. Many parents want to be involved in classroom activities; however, they cannot afford the time away from work to volunteer on a regular basis. Decide how many days a month you want to set aside for guest readers. Then, at Back-to-School Night—or some other time in the fall—provide a sign-up sheet for interested parent guest readers, with the dates for which you are looking for volunteers. Working parents love this idea because they can still participate in a classroom activity; however, their time commitment is defined.

Read-Aloud Activities (cont.)

Repeated Readings

Repeated readings of a text are what help increase a student's ability to read fluently. The challenge for teachers is to provide fun and meaningful ways for students to reread a text. The best way to do this is to provide authentic reasons for students to reread a text. For example, students will be much more willing to reread a Readers Theater script 10 times in order to practice for performing for a kindergarten classroom than they would be if you handed them a book and had them reread the book 10 times. Provided throughout this fluency section are a variety of ways to encourage students to read and reread a text.

Text Sets

There are many children's series appropriate for first grade that provide excellent reading practice. The series listed on page 89 can be used with any of the techniques for encouraging fluency using repeated readings explained throughout this section.

One of the defining features of the series listed below is common characters. Familiarity with the names of the characters encourages recognition when reading the books. For example, in the *Froggy* series of books, Froggy, mother, father, his teacher, Mrs. Witherspoon, and even friends such as Frogilina make an appearance in most of the books. Familiarity with the names of the characters in the books helps students to recognize and read the names when they appear in the text.

Additionally, the characters within a series often use similar vocabulary. For example, in each of the *Froggy* books, there are some words and phrases that are repeated in each of the books. Froggy repeats the word, "Whaaaat!" in each book and he usually ends up eating flies at the end of the book. Students familiar with the *Froggy* series will anticipate these words in the books and are thus prepared to recognize and read the words when they come to them. See page 89 for text sets with similar characters.

The term "text set" does not necessarily have to mean stories with the same character. Text sets can also be books with a similar theme. For example, students comfortable and familiar with reading one book on ants will have a higher degree of success and fluency, due to word familiarity and recognition, when reading additional books on ants. Consider grouping texts into sets that correspond to each other in some way. One way many teachers do this is by placing books together in a basket. For example, during the month of October, place all of the Halloween related stories you have or have checked out from the library together in a basket. Another excellent way to accomplish creating a text set is by the topic you are currently studying. Create a display table with books and objects related to the topic of study.

Books in a Series

Froggy Series by Jonathan London

Froggy Bakes a Cake. Grosset and Dunlap, 2000.

Froggy Eats Out. Viking, 2001.

Froggy Gets Dressed. Vikings Children's Books, 1997.

Froggy Goes to Bed. Puffin, 2002.

Froggy Goes to School. Puffin, 1998.

Froggy Goes to the Doctor. Viking Children's Book, 2002.

Froggy Learns to Swim. Puffin, 1997.

Froggy Plays in the Band. Viking, 2002.

Froggy Plays Soccer. Puffin, 2001.

Froggy's Baby Sister. Viking, 2003.

Froggy's Best Christmas. Puffin, 2002.

Froggy's First Kiss. Puffin, 1999.

Froggy's Halloween. Viking, 1999.

Let's Go Froggy. Puffin, 1996.

Frog and Toad Series by Arnold Loebel

Days with Frog and Toad. Harper Trophy, 1984.

Frog and Toad All Year. Harper Trophy, 1984.

Frog and Toad are Friends. HarperCollins Juvenile Books, 1979.

Frog and Toad Together. Harper Trophy, 1979.

Clifford Series by Norman Bridwell

Clifford Grows Up. Cartwheel Books, 1999.

Clifford the Big Red Dog. Scholastic, 1995.

Clifford the Firehouse Dog. Scholastic, 1994.

Clifford's Bedtime. Scholastic, 1991.

Clifford's Birthday Party. Scholastic, 1990.

Clifford's Family. Cartwheel Books, 1984.

Clifford's First Autumn. Scholastic, 1997.

Clifford's Halloween. Scholastic, 1991.

Clifford's Kitten. Cartwheel Books, 1994.

Clifford's Manners. Scholastic, 1987.

Clifford's Thanksgiving Visit. Cartwheel Books, 1993.

Henry and Mudge Series by Cynthia Rylant

Henry and Mudge and the Forever Sea. Aladdin Library, 1997.

Henry and Mudge and the Happy Cat. Aladdin Library, 1996.

Henry and Mudge and the Long Weekend. Aladdin, 1996.

Henry and Mudge and the Snowman Plan. Aladdin Library, 2000.

Henry and Mudge in Puddle Trouble. Scott Foresman, 1996.

Henry and Mudge in the Sparkle Days. Aladdin, 1997.

Henry and Mudge Take the Big Test. Scott Foresman, 1996.

Henry and Mudge Under the Yellow Moon. Aladdin Library, 1996.

Golly Sisters Series by Betsy Byars

Golly Sisters Go West. HarperTrophy, 1990.

Hooray for the Golly Sisters. HarperCollins Juvenile Books, 1992.

The Golly Sisters Ride Again. HarperTrophy, 1996.

Amelia Bedelia Series by Peggy Parish

Amelia Bedelia and the Surprise Shower. HarperTrophy, 1994.

Amelia Bedelia Helps Out. Harper Trophy, 1997.

Amelia Bedelia. HarperCollins Juvenile Books, 1992.

Come Back Amelia Bedelia. HarperCollins Publishers, 1978.

Good Work Amelia Bedelia. Harper Trophy, 2003.

Play Ball Amelia Bedelia. Harper Trophy, 1978.

Teach Us Amelia Bedelia. Harper Trophy, 2004.

Thank You Amelia Bedelia. Harper Trophy, 2003.

Arthur Series by Marc Brown

Arthur Goes to Camp. Little Brown and Company, 1984.

Arthur Writes a Story. Little Brown and Company, 1998.

Arthur's Birthday. Little Brown and Company, 1991.

Arthur's Chicken Pox. Little Brown and Company, 1996.

Arthur's Family Vacation. Little Brown and Company, 1995.

Arthur's First Sleep Over. Little Brown and Company, 1996.

Arthur's New Puppy. Little Brown and Company, 1995.

Arthur's Teacher Trouble. Little Brown and Company, 1989.

Arthur's Tooth. Little Brown and Company, 1986.

Songs and Poetry

Songs and poetry provide a wonderful resource for students to develop and practice fluency, especially at the beginning of first grade when many students are limited in what they are able to read on their own. By charting songs and poems on poster board or by reproducing the words on a transparency for the overhead projector, students have access to the words of the song or poem. Demonstrate tracking the words by pointing to each word as it is read.

One way fluency is developed is when passages of text are read and reread. The more familiar students are with the words of a text, the less they have to work on decoding the words. Students can devote more time to making the reading sound like natural language. Singing songs, especially, provides an excellent reason for students to read and reread a text. Once students are familiar with a song, they love to sing it again and again. Many students are apt to sing a song many more times than they would reread a book.

Songs and poems lend themselves to good phrasing, too. By practicing the songs and poems, students are practicing the phrasing that naturally comes with singing the song or saying the poem correctly. To demonstrate this point, try reading the familiar nursery rhyme below with the inappropriate phrasing.

One, Two, Buckle My Shoe

One, two, buckle my/
Shoe. Three, four, shut/
The door. Five, six, pick up/
Sticks. Seven, eight, lay/
Them straight. Nine,/
Ten, a big fat hen.

The nursery rhyme feels unnatural to read in this manner because the phrases of the poem do not make sense when grouped in this way. In the same way, once students become familiar with a poem or song, students will begin to get a feel for the natural flow and phrasing of language.

Additional suggestions for using songs and poetry are provided on pages 91 and 92.

Additional Song and Poetry Ideas

- Many classes sing a patriotic song after saying the flag salute each morning. Chart the songs you sing and put them in an accessible place for the children.
- Nursery rhymes provide excellent sources of poetry. Many students are already familiar with the rhymes.
- Traditional hand rhymes are easy for students to learn. The hand movements help students remember the words.

Songs and Poetry (cont.)

Songs on CD

Make use of the CDs you probably have in your classroom for reading and fluency practice. Photocopy the words provided on the insert of the CD case. You may need to enlarge the words if they are printed in a font that is too small. Create transparencies of the words to the songs. Display the words to the songs on the overhead projector before playing the CD. Then, play the CD while you track the words to the song on the overhead.

If desired, you may wish to create song booklets, one for each child, by photocopying all of the words to the songs and stapling them together. If students have their own song booklets, tell them to practice tracking the words to the song while they sing.

As students become familiar with the songs, they are practicing recognizing words more quickly while pointing to the words and singing. Additionally, the song has a rate at which it moves. Because the song is continually moving at that rate, students are forced to keep up with the song while pointing to the words and singing; students are not permitted time to slow down to figure out words. Students hear any words they do not know when the singer of the song sings the words. This helps students to continue to read and not get bogged down on a word.

Children's Poetry Resources

Provided below is a list of excellent poetry resources that can be used to locate poems on topics you are currently studying in your classroom. Poetry from these books can be used as additional texts for topics your class is studying and to help students develop fluency.

Berstein, Joanne E. and Cohen, Paul. *Creepy Crawly Critter Riddles.* Weekly Reader Books, 1986.

Cole, Joanna. *Anna Banana: 101 Jump Rope Rhymes.* William Morrow, 1989.

Cullinan, Bernice. *A Jar of Tiny Stars: Poems by NCTE Award Winning Poets.* Boyds Mills Press, 1996.

de Regniers, B.S. *Sing a Song of Popcorn.* Scholastic, 1988.

Fleichman, Paul and Eric Beddows. *Joyful Noise: Poems for Two Voices.* HarperCollins Juvenile Books, 1992.

Frank, Josette. *Poems to Read to the Very Young.* Random House, 2000.

Prelutsky, Jack. *The New Kid on the Block.* Greenwillow, 1984.

————. *A Pizza the Size of the Sun.* Greenwillow, 1996.

————. *The Random House Book of Poetry for Children.* Random House, 1983.

————. *Read Aloud Rhymes for the Very Young.* Knopf, 1986.

Sevenson, Robert Lewis. *A Child's Garden of Verses.* Franklin Watts, 1966.

Silverstein, Shel. *A Light in the Attic.* HarperCollins Publishers, 1981.

————. *Where the Sidewalk Ends.* HarperCollins Publishers, 1974.

X.J. and Dorothy Kennedy. *Knock at a Star: A Child's Introduction to Poetry.* Little Brown, and Company, 1999.

Songs and Poetry (cont.)

Piggyback Songs

Piggyback songs make excellent fluency practice. Piggyback songs are new songs sung to the tune of a familiar song. For example, new words about the four seasons can be sung to the tune of "Oh My Darling Clementine."

The Four Seasons

(to the tune of "Oh My Darling Clementine")

Winter, spring, summer, fall—
There are four seasons in all.
Winter, spring, summer, fall—
There are four seasons in all.

In the winter, trees are bare.
Snow is falling on the ground.
It is frosty; it is cold.
We have to wear warm clothes.

Springtime's breezy and sometimes rainy.
It is green on the ground and tress.
Baby animals are being born.
There is new growth all around.

Summer's hot and often sweaty—
Lots of time to go swimming.
School is out and it is playtime;
Sunny days are so much fun.

In the fall, leaves are changing;
They are falling on the ground.
It's a cooler type of weather—
Time for harvest and school.

Piggyback songs are excellent for several reasons. First, the songs do not require the teacher or leader to know how to read music. Teachers and students are already familiar with most of the tunes for the songs. The students' familiarity with the tunes helps move the song along, as well as provide proper phrasing for the words of the song. Students love to sing these songs because the tunes are familiar and yet there is a twist to them. Singing provides reading and fluency practice, as well as reasons to continually reread (or in this case re-sing) the words.

Many district resource centers have compilations of piggyback songs available for holidays, as well as a variety of content area and thematic topics. Check with your resource center to see if songs are available to you. There are internet sites devoted to posting piggyback songs teachers have written. Additionally, there are piggyback songs books that are excellent. See the listings below for Internet sites and publishers information.

Internet Resources

- *http://www.pentatonika.com/piggyback.html*
- *http://www.tnfb.com/specialprograms/pages/songs.htm*
- *http://www.umkc.edu/imc/songs.htm*

Publishers Information

Warren, Jean. *Holiday Piggyback Songs.* Warren Publishing House, 1998.

————. *Piggyback Songs for School.* Warren Publishing House, 1991.

————. *Piggyback Songs: New Songs Sung to the Tunes of Childhood Favorites.* Warren Publishing House, 1983.

Student/Adult Reading

Utilize the benefits of an adult modeling how a fluent reader sounds by doing student/adult reading with children. Select a reading passage with which you would like a child to practice fluency. The adult (a teacher, parent, tutor, or even a more fluent peer) reads the passage and a child re-reads the passage. The adult has modeled how to fluently read the passage, as well as any words that may have otherwise been difficult for the student. Repeated re-readings may be necessary for students to fluently read the passage.

This technique is especially useful for modeling how a reader would read a sentence with punctuation (including commas) and ending punctuation (such as exclamation points or question marks). The adult first models the intonation of the passage and students re-read, trying to emulate the same intonation. By hearing how a fluent reader raises and lowers his or her voice or speeds up or slows down when reading, students begin to understand the effect punctuation has on reading a text.

For first-grade students who are not yet reading, especially at the beginning of the school year, you may wish to do echo reading. Echo reading is when a teacher (or other adult) reads a line of text and then has students repeat or echo the same line. Usually in echo reading, the amount of text the students repeat is limited to a sentence or two. Also, because students are not yet reading the text—they are repeating it—use this opportunity to draw their attention to the text. The children should point to the words as you are reading and as they are reading. As you are reading, you are modeling one-to-one correspondence with the words, as well as the left return-sweep. By having students point to the words, too, they are practicing these important concepts of print, as well as attending to the words on the page. Draw students' attention to punctuation, emphasized words (bolded words or words in different fonts), and how those elements in the text affect your reading of it.

Choral Reading

Choral reading is a whole class or a group of students reading together. Choral readings begin with a fluent reader reading the book or passage of text in order to model fluent reading. Then students are encouraged to participate in subsequent re-readings of the text. Depending on the text, some students may chime in on the second reading. Others may still need time to absorb the story line or patterning in the text before they feel comfortable to join. For this reason, and to encourage fluent readings of the text, re-read the text on several occasions, perhaps over several days. Patterned and predictable books are excellent for choral readings. Poetry also works well for choral readings due to the rhythmic nature of poetry, as well as the short length of text. Due to the nature of short poems and patterned and predictable books, students will probably memorize the text. Be sure to continue to display the text and continue to draw attention to it during readings. This emphasizes that the meaning of what is being "read" is coming from the print in the book.

Songs

Build on children's love for singing in order to build fluency. Use songs for choral readings. Piggyback songs (see page 92) in particular are excellent practice for choral reading because the words are new to the children while the tune of the song is familiar. Remember, the children need access to the print, so consider photocopying and distributing the words to each child, writing the words on a piece of chart paper, or displaying the words on an overhead projector.

Group Divisions

Once students are familiar with a text, divide them into groups to re-read. This technique works especially well when there is a repeating line or if one group can echo another group. For example, in the song "Down by the Bay," one group can sing the words, "Down by the bay," while the other group can repeat, "Down by the bay." Continue this echoing for the remainder of the song and then switch which group sings first. Groups can be made using a variety of divisions, boys and girls, children wearing jackets and children not wearing jackets, children who are five and children who are six, etc.

Tape-Assisted Reading

Students can practice fluency by participating in tape-assisted reading. Provide students with an audio tape or CD and book of a text that is at the child's independent reading level. Have students listen to the tape while following along in the book. Then, students should rewind the tape and play the tape again, this time while reading out loud along with the story. Tape and book sets are commercially available; however, consider making your own. The benefits of making your own audio tapes include the ability to use books you already own; being able to use a slower-than-normal reading rate that students can follow easily; and, of course, spending less money. Use books from your classroom, especially patterned or predictable books for first-graders. It is important to note that tape-assisted reading is not listening to a story on an audio tape; however, that activity can be incorporated in your endeavor to read aloud to children. The purpose of tape-assisted reading is as another means of modeling fluent reading to children, and then allowing them to practice reading fluently on a reread of the same material. Nursery rhymes make excellent tape assisted reading, especially at the beginning of the year.

Partner Reading

Pair students to read to each other. The purpose, again, is for fluent reading to be modeled prior to a less fluent reader attempting to read the same passage. There are two ways in which this can be done. First, pair a more fluent reader with a less fluent reader. The fluent reader can model reading a passage, and then the less fluent reader can reread the same passage. Some schools have implemented an upper-grade buddy system in which a whole classroom of third graders, for instance, comes to read with a kindergarten classroom. This type of situation is ideal for having the third graders model fluent reading, and then having the kindergarten students practice. Be sure the books selected for partner reading are appropriate for kindergarten students to practice reading independently. Again, patterned and predictable books are ideal for this situation. Second, pair students with similar reading abilities after receiving the same instruction during a guided or shared reading of a passage. The idea here is that the passage is not new, it has been modeled by a fluent reader. Students then have the opportunity to practice reading the passage fluently.

Make Your Own Books

Books that students participate in making are very motivating for them to read. Additionally, if the books are carefully designed, students will be able to read them, especially at the beginning of the year when some students may be non-readers.

The easiest type of book students can participate in making is a sentence frame book. The teacher provides a sentence frame that each child will use with a blank in which the child can fill in his or her own response. A picture is drawn to correspond to the sentence. For example, the teacher may provide the sentence, "This is a _____." Students can each draw and write in their own response in the blank. For example, a student could write, "This is a car." The student would draw a picture of a car to correspond with the sentence.

You may want to introduce the sentence frame to students and then elicit ideas from them. Chart student responses on a piece of chart paper so they have a reference when they go to work on their own page.

Once all the students have completed their own pages, the student pages can be assembled into a class book that can be placed in the classroom library. Students love to read these types of books and become very fluent because of the repetitive text. Additionally, these books encourage sight-word recognition because students are reading the words over and over and because they are using them in an authentic context.

Encourage students who are capable to copy the entire sentence themselves. If students are unable to copy the sentence, provide the sentence frame for them and encourage the students to fill in the missing word(s). Consider some of the suggestions for cloze sentences below. Simple cloze sentences are especially useful at the beginning of first grade.

This is a _____.

It is a _____.

It is my _____.

I see a _____.

See the _____.

It is a _____.

Can you find the _____?

Here is a _____.

I can _____.

Look at the _____.

I can see the _____.

I see the _____.

Can you see the _____?

I like the _____.

Individual Books

Once students are comfortable with completing one page of a class book, encourage them to create their own book. Use similar cloze sentences, such as those listed above; however, encourage students to complete the entire book themselves. Three examples of individual books are provided on pages 97–99. The cloze sentence pattern remains the same on all the pages. This encourages student familiarity with the words, which leads to reading with better fluency. Students can take these individual books home to practice reading with their families.

I can _____.

I can _____.

I can _____.

My "I Can" Book

Name _____

Look and Find

Can you find the _____?

Name _____

Look
and Find

Can you find the _____?

Can you find the _____?

Things I Can See

<table>
<tr><td>

Name ‾‾‾‾‾‾‾‾‾‾‾‾‾‾

**Things
I Can See**

</td><td>

I can see a ‾‾‾‾‾‾‾‾‾‾.

</td></tr>
<tr><td>

I can see a ‾‾‾‾‾‾‾‾‾‾.

</td><td>

I can see a ‾‾‾‾‾‾‾‾‾‾.

</td></tr>
</table>

Readers Theater

Readers Theater is the reading of a text in a play-like fashion. Although props and costumes can be involved in an elaborate Readers Theater, most involve the children simply reading the text with good fluency. By performing a Readers Theater, students are given an excellent reason to read and reread a text—they are practicing for a performance. Encourage student participation while practicing a Readers Theater script by motivating students with the promise of a performance. Invite another classroom, older book buddies, or even parents in for the performance. Examples of Readers Theaters related to first-grade content areas are provided on pages 101–103.

Create a Readers Theater

It is fun and easy to create your own Readers Theater. Readers Theaters are easy to write, especially with repetitive and patterned books. A teacher or other capable reader will probably need to read the narrator parts that will carry the bulk of the plot. Students can be assigned simple lines or even repetitive or patterned lines. Follow the steps below to create your own Readers Theater.

1. Select a book that you want to adapt to a Readers Theater format.

2. Some people find it easiest to type the entire text and then delete the portions of the text not needed. Other people can edit as they type.

3. Delete lines that repeat who said them. For example, if a line says, "'Run, run as fast as you can, you can't catch me, I'm the Gingerbread Man,' said the Gingerbread Man." Delete the part that says, "said the Gingerbread Man."

4. Delete lines that are not necessary to the plot.

5. Assign lines to characters. Consider if the text from the book is too difficult for the reading abilities of your students. If the text is too difficult, rewrite the lines to simplify the words.

6. Assign lines that explain the plot or setting to the narrator.

7. Practice, practice, practice!

"Run, run as fast as you can, you can't catch me, I'm the Gingerbread Man,' said the Gingerbread Man."

Growing a Plant

Readers Theater

Readers: Student 1, Student 2

Student 1: Dig a little hole.

Student 2: Plant a little seed.

Student 1: Add some sun and water.

Student 2: And wait very patiently.

Student 1: Underneath the ground, the roots will start to grow.

Student 2: After a little while, a stem will start to show.

Student 1: The stem will grow up taller.

Student 2: And leaves begin to form.

Student 1: A bud turns into a flower.

Student 2: That's how a plant is born.

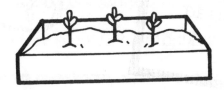

Community Helpers

Readers: Student 1, Student 2

(Alternative: assign parts to eight students, one student each line. All students can read the last four lines together.)

Student 1: A doctor knows how to help me when I'm sick.

Student 2: A construction worker knows just how to lay brick.

Student 1: A firefighter can help put out a fire.

Student 2: A mechanic knows how to fix a flat tire.

Student 1: A delivery by mail comes by the mailman.

Student 2: A grocer's job is to stock the store with cans.

Student 1: A teacher's job is to teach and teach and teach.

Student 2: A lifeguard keeps kids safe along the beach.

Student 1: All these jobs are needed to help a community run.

Student 2: If workers do their jobs, all the work will be done.

Student 1: There is a perfect job, just for you.

Student 2: What kind of job would you like to do?

Weather

Readers: Student 1, Student 2

Student 1: If the weather's warm and the sun's already out. . .

Student 2: You can dress in shorts and sandals, you don't have to doubt.

Student 1: If the weather's damp and it looks like it might rain. . .

Student 2: You better wear your raincoat, to watch the water go down the drain.

Student 1: If the weather's cold and it looks like it might snow. . . .

Student 2: Wear your hat and mittens, so snowballs you can throw.

Student 1: If the weather's cool and the wind is starting to blow. . .

Student 2: You better wear pants and a sweater, before outside you go.

Student 1: If you watch the weather, I'm sure that you will find. . .

Student 2: That you will know just what to wear and you will be just fine.

Record a Story

Have students make a tape or CD recording of a book that they are currently reading. The motivation of creating their own recording will encourage students to reread the book, increasing their fluency when reading it. The recording of the book makes an excellent gift for the holidays, Mother's Day, Father's Day, or simply any day! Another idea is to give the book and the recording to a kindergarten class to place in their listening center.

Help the child select a book that is at an appropriate reading level. Have the child practice reading it alone several times. Then, have the child practice reading it with a partner or a small group. The group should be encouraged to provide feedback. Students can make suggestions about intonations, voice tones, pauses that reflect the mood of the book, and any other suggestions that will make the recording truly special. Once the student is comfortable with the way in which he or she reads the book, set up a time to make the recording. You may want to have the reader go to another room or make the recording during recess or lunch to minimize the distractions and background noise on the recording.

Then, photocopy the pattern below. You may want to photocopy it onto cardstock paper for durability. Allow the students to decorate the pattern as the cover to the tape box. Be sure to remind students to include the name of the book and the person making the recording. Place the cover and the tape in the cassette box. If the recording will be given as a gift, wrap the box or tie it with a bow.

Sight-Word Activities

Sight words are words students should recognize instantly due to the high frequency with which they occur in written materials. Many of the high frequency words are words that cannot be sounded out. Recognizing these words instantly leads to more fluent reading. Students are not stumbling over these words, rather, they are recognizing and reading the words quickly and accurately and moving on to read the next word. See page 107 for a list of high frequency words. Listed below are some activities that can be used to help students increase the number of sight words they recognize.

Word of the Day

Make a sight word a "word of the day" each day. Save name badge holders from conferences you attend. Write the sight word of the day on a piece of cardstock or a piece of paper. Place the word in the name badge holder and wear it around during the day. On the reverse side of the word you may wish to draw a picture for students to associate with the word or use the word in a sentence. Encourage students to read the word when waiting in line for lunch, recess, or on their way out the door on the way home. Add the sight word to your word wall after you have worn it around for the day.

Ring of Words

Provide each student with a 2" ring. Cut 3" x 5" index cards in half to create 3" x 2.5" cards. Hole-punch the cards and place a stack on each child's ring. Have students write the sight word each day on a new card. Students can practice reading their word rings in their spare time. Depending on the ability levels of your students, you may want them to write a sentence using the word on the back of the card.

Printing Practice

Use sight words as words for a printing lesson. Rather than running off printing practice worksheets, demonstrate on an overhead transparency correct letter formation and placement, and then have students practice writing the words on a sheet of lined paper. As you write the words, have students spell the words with you. Then elicit sentences from the students using the sight words in them.

Sight-Word Activities (cont.)

Sight-Word Rhyming Words

Help children practice sight words on your word wall and rhyming words at the same time. Determine a sight word on the word wall you want students to identify and practice reading. Then, tell students a word that rhymes with the word you are thinking of from the word wall. For example, if you want students to identify the word *to*, you may give the clue, "I am thinking of a sight word from the word wall that rhymes with *shoe*."

Sight-Word Letter Search

Save junk mail and advertisements sent to your house. Place them in a shallow box in the classroom. Post a sign with the sight words you want students to make using the junk mail and advertisements. Also provide either a piece of chart paper for a whole class chart or pieces of paper for individual or group activities. Have students search for and cut out letters that make up the sight words on the sign. The letters can be from different advertisements and can even be in different fonts and sizes. Students should glue the letters in order to form the sight words. Students can also look for the sight words within the advertisements. If they find the word intact, they can simply cut it out and glue it to the piece of construction paper. This activity makes a great learning center.

Walk the Room

Punch out footprint die cuts or photocopy the pattern at the bottom of this page and cut it out. Write sight words on the footprint shape and tape to the ground. Students will inevitably begin walking the room while reading the words on the footprints.

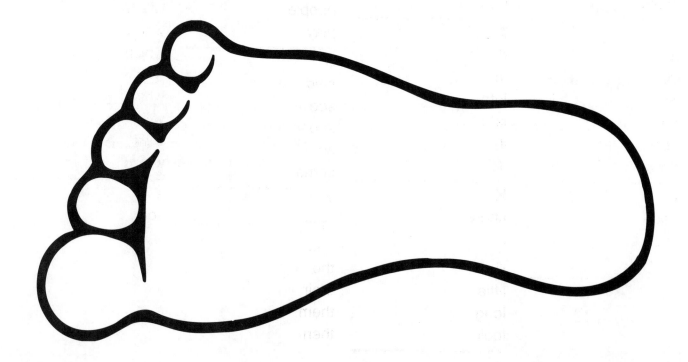

Sight Words

A
a
about
all
am
an
and
are
as
at

B
be
because
been
but
by

C
can
come
could

D
day
did
do
does
done
down

E
each
ever
every

F
find
first
for
from

G
get
go
good

H
had
has
have
he
help
her
here
him
his
how

I
if
in
into
is
it
its

K
know

L
like
little
long
look

M
make
many
me
more
my

N
never
no
not
now

O
of
on
once
one
or
out

P
people
play

S
said
see
she
so
some

T
than
that
the
their
them
then

there
these
they
this
to
too
two

U
up
use

V
very

W
was
way
we
went
were
what
where
when
which
who
why
will
with
would

Y
you
your

Vocabulary

We use words in order to communicate, both in writing and orally. The words we know and use are our vocabulary. A rich vocabulary allows students to be effective communicators and readers. Our goal as teachers is to increase students' vocabularies in order to help them communicate more effectively, as well as for them to more fully understand others. Students can display their rich vocabularies in both speaking and writing. Students also apply their vocabulary when reading. A rich vocabulary background leads to better reading comprehension.

Children learn new vocabulary words two ways, directly and indirectly. Most of the vocabulary students acquire is learned indirectly. Through a variety of literacy events, such as conversing with others and listening to stories, students learn new vocabulary words and how to use them. Direct vocabulary instruction is explicitly teaching a specific word, including defining the word and showing how it is used. Through direct vocabulary instruction, students are able to hear the target word used in a variety of contexts and are provided with opportunities to practice using the word.

Although students do not learn most of their new vocabulary words through direct instruction, direct vocabulary instruction is particularly important for several reasons. First, the teacher is able to introduce specialized vocabulary. If the class will be studying a unit on matter, students need to know specialized science vocabulary words (such as *solid*, *liquid*, and *gas*) that they may not have been exposed to previously. By providing direct instruction on the words *solid*, *liquid*, and *gas*, students will have a better understanding of these terms, as well as the related science concepts, as they are used throughout the science unit. Second, direct vocabulary instruction includes modeling and practicing how words are used in sentences. Although a student may be able to provide a definition for a word, students gradually incorporate vocabulary words into their speaking, reading, and writing vocabularies. This happens as students' understanding of the word is deepened. Finally, students gain a better understanding of the variety of contexts in which a particular word can be used. It is important to note that students are constantly learning the depth of a word as it is used in a variety of contexts.

castle

The vocabulary portion of this books contains four sections: Word Selection, Teaching Vocabulary, Vocabulary Activities, and Categorizing and Classifying. The Word Selection and Teaching Vocabulary sections provide ideas for ways to introduce, teach, and review vocabulary words and concepts. Vocabulary Activities provides vocabulary related activity sheets for topics usually taught in the first grade. Finally, Categorizing and Classifying provides ideas for ways students can see the relationship of one word to another.

Selecting Vocabulary Words

Because children learn the depth of a word based on various encounters with the word, it is important to select words with which students will have a number of exposures to in a short period of time. (See the suggestions below for a variety of ways to select words.) It is recommended that no more than ten vocabulary words be formally introduced in a week, nor more than five at one time. Because the number is limited, be selective when considering words to use. Also, select the number of words based on the amount of time you have to devote to teaching the words.

Once the words have been selected, locate other materials such as books, posters, songs, charts, or diagrams that contain the vocabulary. Seeing the vocabulary again in another context is not only exciting for students, but reinforces the word which helps them build their understanding of the word. For all of the suggestions for selecting vocabulary, it is important to keep in mind that the vocabulary must be meaningful to the student. Select words the student can immediately incorporate into his or her vocabulary. Repeated practice hearing the word in a variety of contexts will help students become more comfortable with their knowledge of the word and thus begin to use it in their everyday conversations.

Topical

Words can be selected based on a unit of study. Teach vocabulary words from a thematic unit of study or from curricular areas of study such as science, social studies, math, or even health or P.E. For example, if you will be teaching a unit on weather, it is an excellent time to introduce words such as *sprinkle*, *downpour*, and *tornado*. Preview the materials you will be using to teach in order to select appropriate words.

Literature Selection

Consider selecting words from a piece of literature that you will be studying or even just reading aloud. Students' comprehension of the text will increase as they will understand more words from the literature.

Grouping Words

Students can develop a better understanding of vocabulary words when similar words are grouped together. For example, when reading the story *Make Way for Ducklings*, it is helpful for students to have an understanding of some of the geography terms used such as pond, river, and island. Although there are many other vocabulary words that could be selected from this book, by selecting geography related terms, students will be able to learn the terms in relationship to the other words, as well as how they are individually used in the book.

Selecting Vocabulary Words (cont.)

Opposites

Students who have a good understanding of antonyms can benefit from vocabulary words that are opposites. For example, if you wanted to use the vocabulary word *ill*, you may also select the word *well*. By using both words as vocabulary words, they can be compared and contrasted so students can get a fuller sense of the meaning of each word. This is an especially useful strategy when students are already very familiar with one of the words.

Multiple Meanings

Enrich students' vocabularies by selecting words with multiple meanings. To begin with, it is suggested that you select words for which students already know one meaning. For example, students already know the meaning of the word *foot*. It is that body part at the end of your leg, right? But, what about the foot of a ladder, the foot of a bed, the foot on a piece of furniture, or the unit of measurement? These are all ways in which the word *foot* can be used.

Synonyms

Synonyms are excellent words to use for vocabulary instruction. We often use a variety of words to say the same thing. Think about the words we can use to say *sad*: *blue*, *upset*, *melancholy*, *gloomy*. Teach students a variety of ways to say words they use in their everyday speaking.

Distinction Words

There are often a variety of ways to say a word, and the word choice we make can add distinction. For example, students understand the sentence, "It is raining outside." Introduce students to the distinctions we can make about how hard it is raining. For example, we use these words to explain rain: *sprinkling, pouring, drizzling,* and *misting*. Introduce students to words that add distinction in order to make the ways in which the word is used more specific.

Words Encountered in Worksheets

There are many words we take for granted that students understand. Take a look at words from your phonics program and consider some of those words for vocabulary words. There are many CVC (consonant, vowel, consonant) words students are expected to read, and yet we never spend more than a second or two explaining them. For example, *nip, gap,* and *den* are not unusual for first-graders to encounter; however, many students do not have a good understanding of the definitions of these words.

Selecting Vocabulary Words (cont.)

Location Words

In, on, around—although these words may seem simple and students have undoubtedly heard them used before, location words are tough words for many first-grade students to fully grasp and use appropriately. Consider identifying location words that you have noticed students have had a difficult time using appropriately and using these words as vocabulary words in order to deepen student understanding of how these terms can be used.

School Events

There are many events in which students participate at school that generate rich opportunities to develop vocabulary. For example, have your students ever carefully considered the word *assembly*? Think about the regularly scheduled and specially scheduled events in which your students participate. You may even want to consider events that students may have heard about through older siblings but are not yet old enough to participate in. For example, a first-grader may not be on the track team; however, he or she may be curious what a track meet is.

Idioms

Students don't usually encounter a formal study of idioms until later in their schooling years; however, consider including idioms as vocabulary terms as they relate to topics of study. For example, if you are studying a unit on weather, in addition to the words *sprinkle, downpour,* and *tornado,* consider adding the term, "It's raining cats and dogs."

Familiar Words

Not all vocabulary words have to be new. Study familiar words, too. Students enjoy being able to recognize words and participate in sharing their meanings. By including words familiar to students, you may be able to expand students' understanding of how the word can be used.

Holiday Related

There are many holiday-related words with which students may not be familiar, especially for terms that are used only once a year. Consider upcoming holidays and select vocabulary words based on themes of the holiday. For example, for St. Patrick's Day, you may select vocabulary terms such as *leprechaun, blarney stone, "top of the day,"* or *shamrock.*

Words that Sound Similar

Do you have students in your class that think that in the alphabet song, the letters *L, M, N, O,* and *P* are all one word, LMNOP? Or students who think *drawer* and *door* are the same word? Without direct instruction, there are many words that sound similar to students until distinctions are made. As these words come up in your classroom, add them to your vocabulary list. By providing instruction in how these words sound different and look different when we spell and read them, students gain an understanding of both of the words.

Teaching Vocabulary

Use a Rich Vocabulary

This may be like stating the obvious; however, teachers can do a lot to improve student vocabulary by being conscious of using a rich vocabulary throughout the day and throughout the year. At the beginning of each month, select several words you would like to incorporate into your everyday language. See "Selecting Vocabulary Words" on pages 109–111 for ideas for selecting vocabulary. For example, you may want students to be aware of the term *wastebasket*. Substitute the word *wastebasket* for *trash can* every opportunity you have to do so.

Read-Alouds

Most teachers are already aware of the far-reaching benefits of read-alouds, but it still is important to at least mention reading books aloud as an important way to develop vocabulary. By hearing books read out loud, students are provided with examples of rich vocabulary used in a variety of sentences and contexts. An especially useful strategy is to select books related to topics currently being studied or to select vocabulary from the books being read. See "Selecting Vocabulary Words" on pages 109–111. Students gain a better understanding of words as they hear them repeatedly and in a variety of contexts.

Realia

Bring objects from home into the classroom. By seeing and touching an object, students are more likely to remember both the vocabulary word, as well as other information about the object.

> *Literature-based*—Bring an object related to a piece of literature that is being read in class. For example, bring a stone to school when reading the book *Stone Soup*. Either prior to or after reading the story, discuss the word *stone*. How is a stone different and the same as a rock? Relating a piece of realia to a story helps to develop vocabulary, as well as helping students to remember the story better.
>
> *Curriculum-based*—Consider areas in the curriculum from which you can bring a piece of realia. For example, if you are studying plants, bring a variety of types of plants for students to look at. Many children have never seen a cactus or a Venus fly trap. Observing and learning about these plants helps students understand more about the characteristics of plants and provides first-hand knowledge of these terms.
>
> *Usual and Unusual Objects*—There are many objects with which students may have had limited experiences, such as pin cushions or coconuts. Many of the objects can be found right in your own home or easily obtained from, for example, a grocery store.

Teaching Vocabulary (cont.)

Picture/Word Dictionary

This method of vocabulary instruction is particularly useful when introducing vocabulary students will encounter, perhaps in a book. Select several (usually no more than five) vocabulary words which you want to introduce to students. The words do not necessarily have to relate to each other; however, it is helpful to students if they do. For example, when reading the story *Make Way for Ducklings*, it is helpful for students to have an understanding of some of the geography terms used such as *pond, river,* and *island*. If many of the vocabulary words will be new to students, it is nice to include at least one word with which students are already familiar. Photocopy and distribute page 114 to each student. You may wish to do the activity with students on an overhead transparency of the page. Write a vocabulary word at the bottom of each square and then as you explain the word to the students, draw a simple illustration to correspond. Students should also write the word and draw a picture on their own paper. Students will have a better understanding of the words when they encounter them in the text.

Quarter a Word

Chose a word to "quarter" together as a class or small group. Fold a piece of construction paper into four sections or draw a rectangle on the whiteboard and divide it into four sections by drawing lines. In the first section, write the vocabulary word. In the second section, write a definition of the word. The definition can either be looked up in the dictionary or defined by the students. The third section contains a picture of the word. The picture can either be drawn or cut out of an old magazine. The final section includes a sentence that demonstrates how the word is used.

Vocabulary Word	Definition
magnet	a piece of iron or steel that attracts certain metals
Picture	**Sentence**
	I picked up the paper clips with a magnet.

Picture/Word Dictionary

Vocabulary

by _____

Cloze Activities

Cloze activities are an excellent way to practice applying vocabulary words. In cloze activities, key words of a sentence are left blank, covered up, or blocked out. Students must use the context of the sentence in order to appropriately fill in the missing word.

Cloze activities can be used to introduce vocabulary words; however, they work best when students are familiar with the words, and more review and application is needed. It is suggested that other strategies be used for introducing the vocabulary words and then cloze activities can be used to review and apply the target words. There are several cloze activities that can be used for developing vocabulary.

Introducing Words

Cloze procedures for introducing vocabulary work best if the vocabulary words do not relate to each other, especially if students are not at all familiar with the words. Students can practice using the context of the sentence in order to determine the word that best completes the sentence. For example, if the vocabulary words you are introducing are *herd*, *bow*, and *stork* from the story *Bringing the Rain to Kapiti Plain*, the following cloze sentences could be used:

- The _____ stood on one foot.
- The _____ of elephants protected the baby elephant.
- I used my _____ and arrow to shoot the target.

Review in Context

Review vocabulary words in the context of several related sentences or a small paragraph. This strategy works especially well when several vocabulary words have been selected that relate to each other. For example, if vocabulary words related to the science topic "Insects" have been selected, provide a cloze activity in which all of the words are connected, such as in a paragraph.

Vocabulary Words		
body	head	legs
thorax	arthropods	abdomen

Insects are _____. All insects have six _____. Insects have three _____ parts. The body parts are called the _____, the _____, and the _____.

Consider using a simple paragraph from a related book or story that includes the vocabulary. Copy the sentences onto sentence strips or chart paper, deleting the key vocabulary words to create cloze sentences. By introducing related vocabulary and then having students practice the vocabulary in cloze procedures such as the one described above, students are able to practice reading the words in context, while developing a better sense of how the words relate to each other.

Cloze Activities (cont.)

Multiple Answers

You may wish to design cloze sentences to work with a variety of related vocabulary words on which you are working. For example, if students are learning about community helpers, a sentence such as, "A _____ is a community worker," may be used to demonstrate how a number of vocabulary words will work within the same context. Students can try a variety of community helpers in the sentence in order to see if all make sense.

- ➢ A *firefighter* is a community worker.
- ➢ A *police officer* is a community worker.
- ➢ A *trash collector* is a community worker.
- ➢ A *mayor* is a community worker.

Reveal a Letter

Occasionally, students will have a difficult time determining the missing word in a cloze sentence, or, as in the activity above, multiple answers may apply to a particular sentence. A good way to help students determine the missing word is to reveal the first letter of the missing word. This will often provide students with enough information to help them determine the word. Depending on the word, you may need to reveal several letters. For example, if the word beings with a blend, you may wish to reveal the first two to three letters for an added clue.

Strategies for Using Cloze Activities

Whiteboard/Chart Paper—The easiest way to use this technique is to simply write the cloze sentence on the whiteboard or chart paper with a blank where the missing word belongs. This requires no preparation and can be done spontaneously as appropriate within your class schedule.

Sentence Strips—Write the cloze sentences on sentence strips. Leave a blank where the missing word belongs. Place the sentence strips in a pocket chart. Vocabulary words can be written on index cards and used in the blanks. This strategy is particularly useful for trying a variety of vocabulary words within each sentence. Doing so helps students understand how context relates to vocabulary. Additionally, the process of elimination can be demonstrated for determining the correct word.

Peek-a-Boos—Consider using sticky notes to cover up key words. Use sentences from any text used in teaching such as songs, poems, big books, posters, and sentence strips. When the correct missing word is determined, reveal the completed sentence by removing the sticky note.

More Vocabulary Activities

True/False

True/False is an excellent game to play with students in order to review vocabulary. Think of several statements about a vocabulary word you want to review. Some of the statements should be true and some should be false. Read the statements to the children, one at a time. Students must determine if the statement is true or false. For example, for the vocabulary word *galoshes* the following statements could be made.

> ➤ I wore my galoshes to school when it rained. (*True*)
> ➤ Mom made galoshes for dinner. (*False*)
> ➤ Her galoshes kept her feet dry. (*True*)
> ➤ Tim keeps his galoshes near his raincoat. (*True*)
> ➤ We grew galoshes in the garden. (*False*)

Determine movements students can perform if a statement is true and other movements if the statement is false. For example, if the statement is true, students can smile. If the statement is false, students can frown. True/False can also be turned into a game by dividing students into teams and having them compete against each other. Keep score to determine a winning team.

Five Senses

Help students develop a fuller understanding of a word by using their five senses. Bring to school an object related to a vocabulary word. Obviously, this activity will need to be modified if an object cannot be tasted. Create a chart on which to record student observations. A column for each sense that will be used should be included. Label each column with one of the five senses. Allow students to observe the object. Record their findings on the chart.

Coconut				
Sight 👁	Touch ✋	Hearing 👂	Smell 👃	Taste 👅
round brown	hard hairy fuzzy	watery liquid		sweet

Location Words

Directions: Cut out the picture cards at the bottom of the page. Follow the directions to determine the location of each picture card. Glue the picture cards in place.

- The eel is next to the cave.
- The octopus is above the seaweed.
- The clam is to the right of the seaweed.
- The crab is by the clam.
- The fish is above the clam.

Synonyms

Directions: Cut out the word circles at the bottom of the page. Glue the word circles on top of the cones to show words that are synonyms.

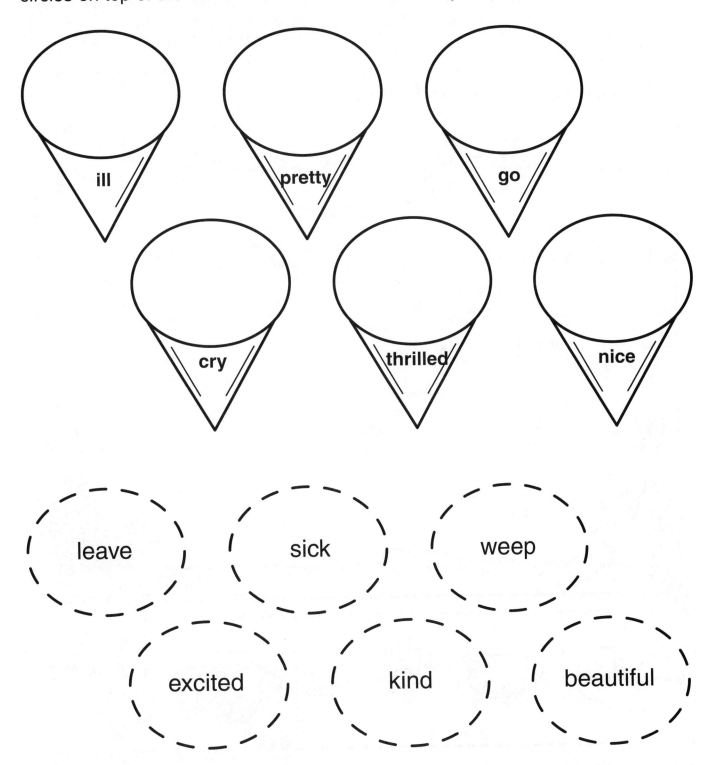

Means the Same

Directions: Cut out the word flaps at the bottom of the page. Put a small amount of glue on the glue tabs on the boxes in the sentences. Match the word flaps to the word boxes that are synonyms. Place the word flaps on top of the glue tabs so that they can be lifted to reveal the words underneath.

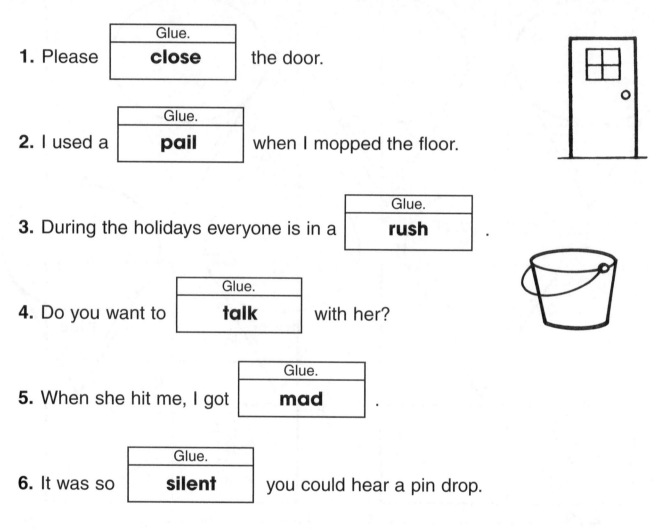

1. Please | Glue. **close** | the door.

2. I used a | Glue. **pail** | when I mopped the floor.

3. During the holidays everyone is in a | Glue. **rush** | .

4. Do you want to | Glue. **talk** | with her?

5. When she hit me, I got | Glue. **mad** | .

6. It was so | Glue. **silent** | you could hear a pin drop.

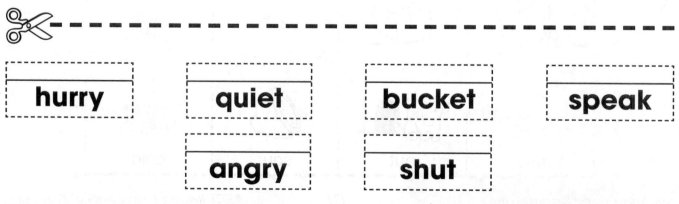

hurry   **quiet**   **bucket**   **speak**

angry   **shut**

Opposites

Directions: Cut out the word/picture cards at the bottom of the page. Glue the word/picture cards in the boxes at the top of the page to show opposites.

1.
old

5.
happy

2.
sweet

6.
open

3.
in

7.
big

4.
run

8.
hot

young   closed   small   walk

sad   out   sour   cold

Just the Opposite

Directions: Cut out the word flaps at the bottom of the page. Place a small amount of glue on the glue tabs on the boxes in the sentences. Match the word flaps to show antonyms. Place the word flaps on top of the glue tabs so that the flaps can be lifted to reveal the word beneath. Read the sentences both ways.

1. The box was | Glue. **full** | .

2. I thought the test was | Glue. **easy** | .

3. The movie made me | Glue. **cry** | .

4. The dog was very | Glue. **old** | .

5. She wore a | Glue. **black** | skirt.

6. We rode the elevator | Glue. **up** | to the third floor.

✂ -

| **young** | **white** | **hard** | **empty** |

| **laugh** | **down** |

Synonyms and Antonyms

Directions: Cut out the word cards at the bottom of the page. Read each word in the chart. Glue a word card to show the synonym and antonym of each word in the chart.

Word	Synonym	Antonym
1. begin		
2. smile		
3. cry		
4. close		
5. mad		
6. over		

start	laugh	frown
above	end	happy
grin	weep	open
shut	angry	under

Same Word

Directions: Cut out the picture cards at the bottom of the page. Glue the picture cards in the boxes to show two meanings for each of the words listed.

1.

bowl	

4.

saw	

2.

pot	

5.

top	

3.

bat	

6.

orange	

Different Meanings

Directions: Cut out the word cards at the bottom of the page. Glue the word cards in the correct places to complete the sentences. Use the context of the sentence to help you determine the meaning of the word.

1. We [   ] do it if we work together.

2. I was a butterfly in the class [   ] .

3. Turn [   ] on Elm Street.

4. I caught a [   ] .

5. She wears mittens when it is [   ] .

6. Jose went outside to [   ] .

7. We [   ] the dog in the backyard.

8. Mom opened a [   ] of beans.

play	left	can	cold
cold	can	left	play

Community Workers

Directions: Cut out the word cards at the bottom of the page. Match the word cards to the correct person at the top of the page.

1.

2.

3.

4.

5.

6.

7.

8.

9.

construction worker	crossing guard	mail carrier
chef	doctor	police officer
sanitation worker	teacher	firefighter

Transportation

Directions: Cut out the word cards at the bottom of the page. Glue the word cards to match the type of transportation.

1.

2.

3.

4.

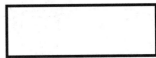

5.

6.

7.

8.

car	ship	train	bus
spaceship	truck	motorcycle	airplane

Shelter

Directions: Cut out the word cards at the bottom of the page. Glue the word cards to match the types of shelter at the top of the page.

1.

2.

3.

4.

5.

6.

igloo	hut	tipi
house	castle	apartment

Clothing Needs

Directions: Cut out the word cards at the bottom of the page. Glue the word cards to match the same type of clothing at the top of the page.

1.

bathing suit

2.

shirt

3.

tennis shoes

4.

pants

5.

coat

6.

dress

7.

sweater

8.

pajamas

| pullover | sleepwear | top | trousers |
| sneakers | frock | swimsuit | jacket |

Places in the Community

Directions: Cut out the word cards at the bottom of the page. Glue the word cards to match the community locations at the top of the page.

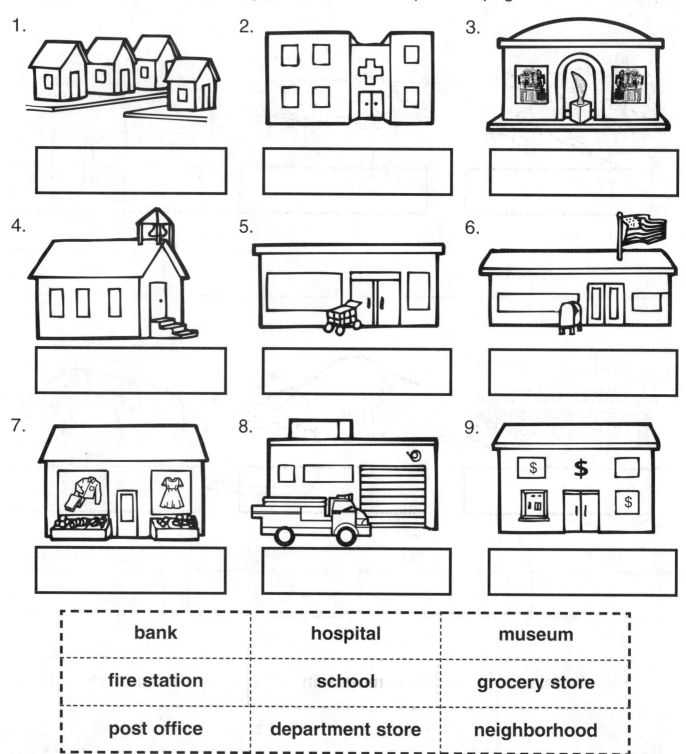

bank	hospital	museum
fire station	school	grocery store
post office	department store	neighborhood

Geography

Directions: Cut out the word cards at the bottom of the page. Glue the word cards in the correct boxes to name the geography features at the top of the page.

1.

2.

3.

4.

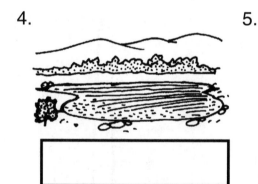

5.

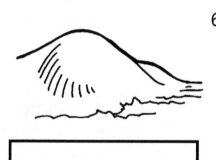

6.

hill	lake	river
island	mountain	ocean

American Symbols

Directions: Cut out the word cards at the bottom of the page. Glue the word cards in the correct boxes to match the American symbols at the top of the page.

1.

2.

3.

4.

5.

6.

| Liberty Bell | Statue of Liberty | Lincoln Memorial |
| American flag | Washington Monument | bald eagle |

Town or Country

Directions: Cut out the word/picture cards at the bottom of the page. Glue each word/picture card in the correct column to show if it belongs in a town or in the country.

Town	Country

cow   apartment   barn   store

taxi   tractor   garage   pig

Parts of a Plant

Directions: Cut out the word cards at the bottom of the page. Glue the word cards in the correct places to show the parts of a plant.

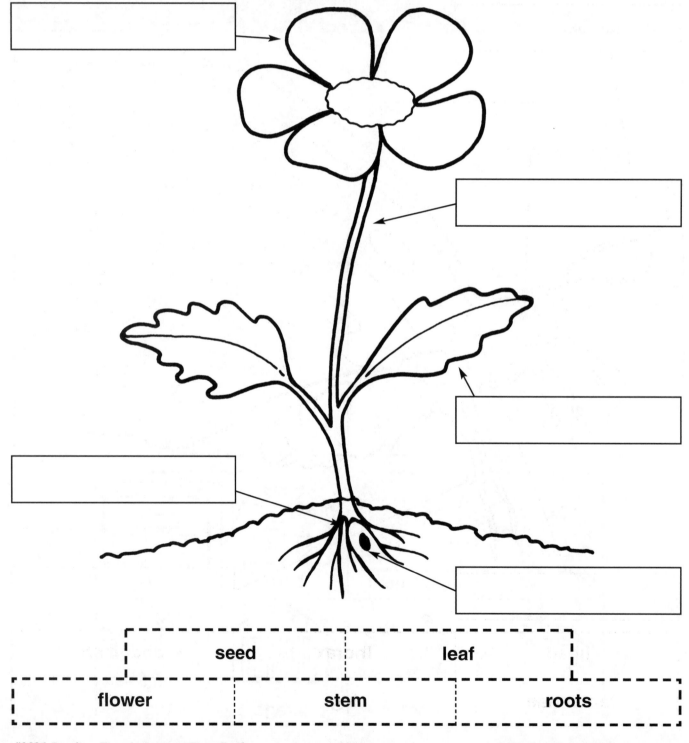

seed   leaf

flower   stem   roots

Parts of a Butterfly

Directions: Cut out the word cards at the bottom of the page. Glue the word cards in the correct places to show the parts of a butterfly.

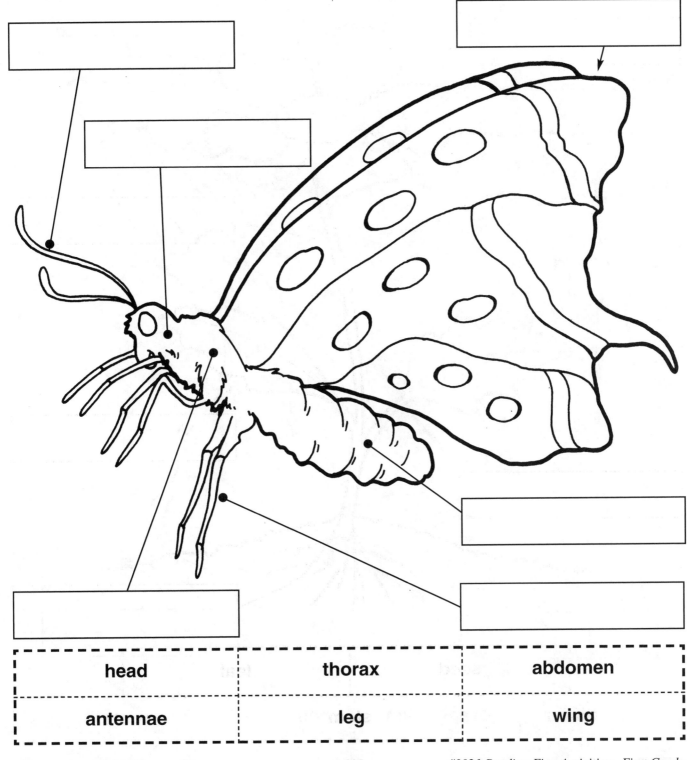

head	thorax	abdomen
antennae	leg	wing

The Water Cycle

Directions: Cut out the word cards at the bottom of the page. Glue the word cards in the correct places to show the water cycle.

| run-off | evaporation | condensation | rain |

Forms of Matter

Directions: Cut out the picture cards at the bottom of the page. Glue the picture cards in the correct columns to show the forms of matter.

Solid	Liquid	Gas

Body Coverings

Directions: Cut out the picture cards at the bottom of the page. Glue the picture cards in the correct columns to show the type of body covering for each animal.

Feathers	Fur	Scales

Tools for Measurement

Directions: Cut out the word cards at the bottom of the page. Glue the word cards in the correct boxes to label the tools for measurement.

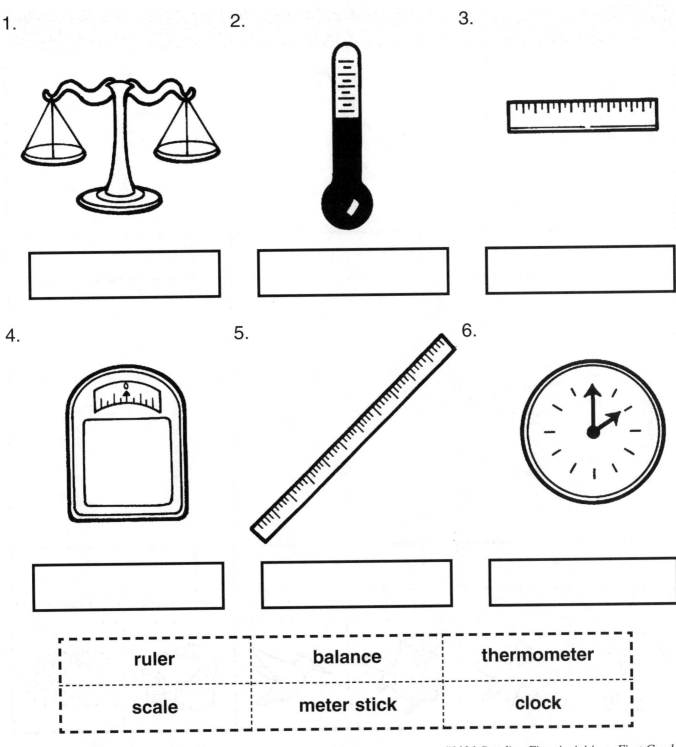

ruler	balance	thermometer
scale	meter stick	clock

Geometric Shapes

Directions: Cut out the word cards at the bottom of the page. Glue the word cards in the correct boxes to show geometric shapes.

1.

2.

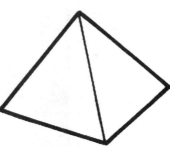

3.

4.

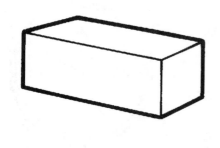

5.

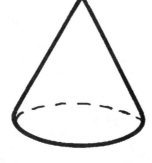

6.

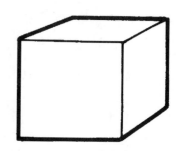

cube	rectangular prism	sphere
cylinder	cone	pyramid

Paint by Color

Directions: Learn about unusual color names. Color the spaces on the art pallet the color indicated on the paint dab.

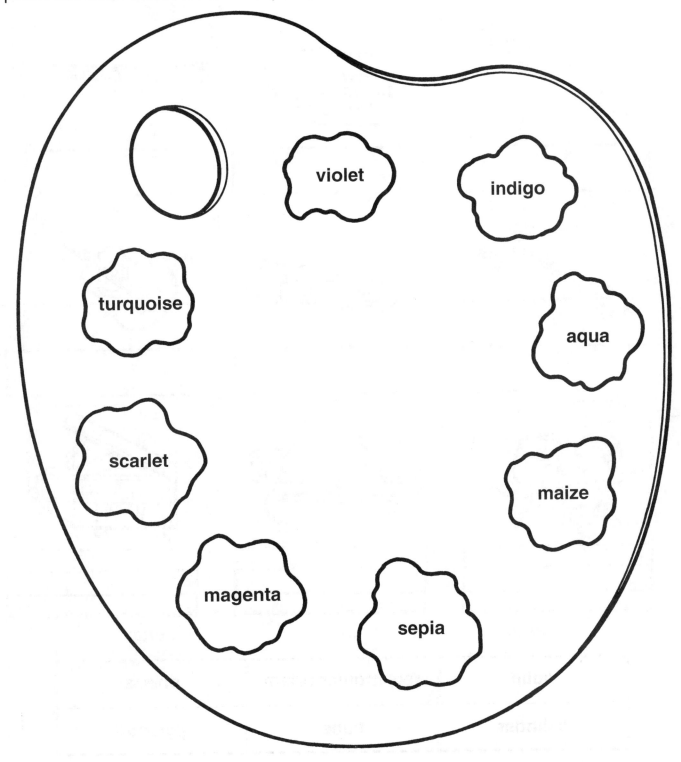

Tune Up

Directions: Cut out the word cards at the bottom of the page. Glue the word cards in the correct boxes to label the instruments.

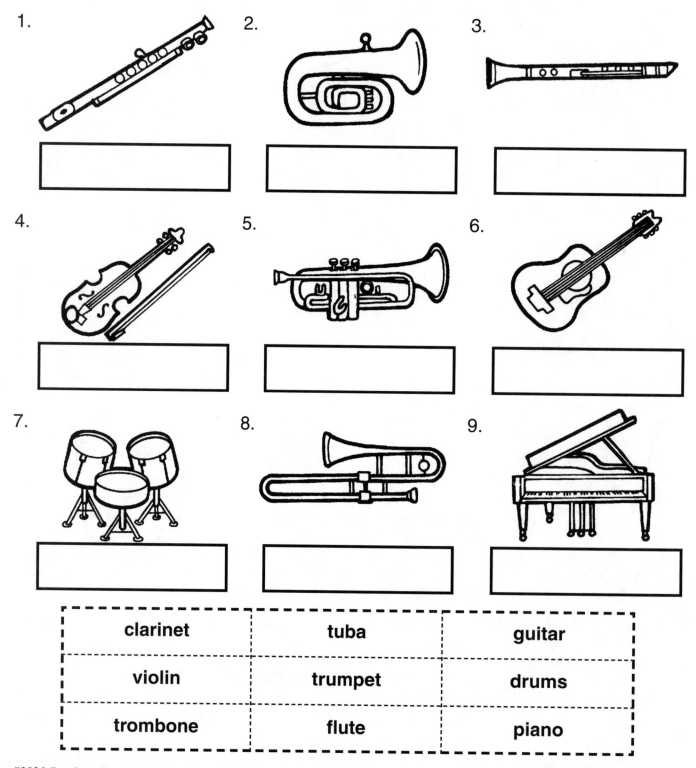

1.

2.

3.

4.

5.

6.

7.

8.

9.

clarinet	tuba	guitar
violin	trumpet	drums
trombone	flute	piano

Classifying and Categorizing Activities

Classifying and categorizing are important vocabulary-building activities. Students build on their understanding of how words are used, as well as the relationship of one word to another. Below are several categorizing and classifying activities that can be done with students.

Category Game

Have children practice naming items in a category by playing the Category Game. Photocopy pages 144–147 onto cardstock paper. Color and laminate the game board (pages 144 and 145), if desired. Cut out the Category Cards (pages 146 and 147). You will need a die and markers—such as buttons or math manipulatives—to play this game.

Directions: Place the Category Game Cards facedown. Roll to see who goes first. The first person rolls the die and moves the number of spaces indicated. Follow the directions for the space the marker lands on. If the student must pick a card, follow the directions on the card. If the student successfully completes the directions on the card, he or she can roll again the next turn. If not, he or she must remain on the space until the task has been successfully completed. The first person to the finish line wins.

Another idea is to use the Category Cards from the game for those five minutes before the recess bell rings. Read a card and have students think of as many words that fit in the category as they can.

Category Clip

Post a large sheet of butcher paper on the wall. Label it with a category. Provide students with a variety of magazines and or newspapers through which to search. The children must find pictures that fit within the category posted. Consider making this a literacy center activity. Have students place their pictures on a large sheet of construction paper rather than a piece of chart paper. Then, assemble the construction paper into a class book.

Categorize It

Once students are skilled at naming items in a category, reverse the teacher/student roles. In this activity, the teacher names the items and the students must name the category. For example, if the teacher said, "Penny, nickel, dime, quarter." Students should respond that the category is "money" or "coins." Sometimes, there will be more than one title that can be given for the words listed. Discuss the options and decide if one title is more appropriate or specific than the other.

Classifying and Categorizing Activity Sheets

Use the activity sheets on pages 148–152 as a way to provide additional practice in categorizing and classifying. The activity sheets range from simple categorizing exercises to more complex and open-ended categorizing and classifying exercises.

Category Game Board

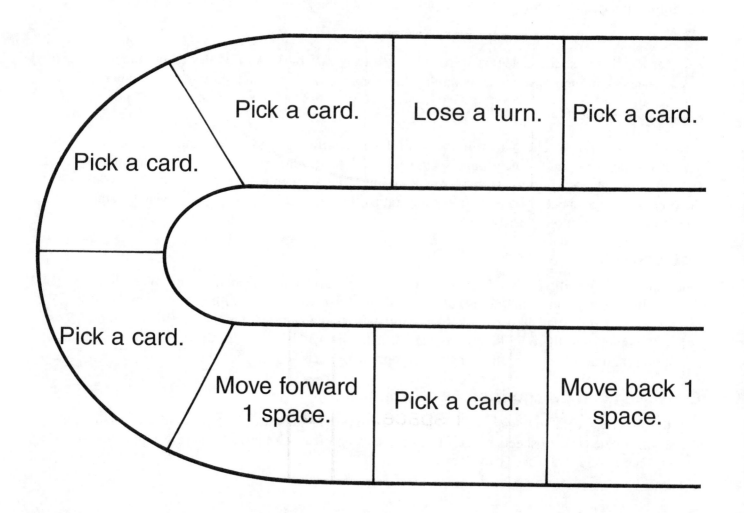

| Start | Move forward 2 spaces. | Pick a card. | Pick a card. | Pick a card. |

| Pick a card. | Pick a card. | Lose a turn. | Pick a card. |

| Pick a card. | Move forward 1 space. | Pick a card. | Move back 1 space. |

Category Game Board (cont.)

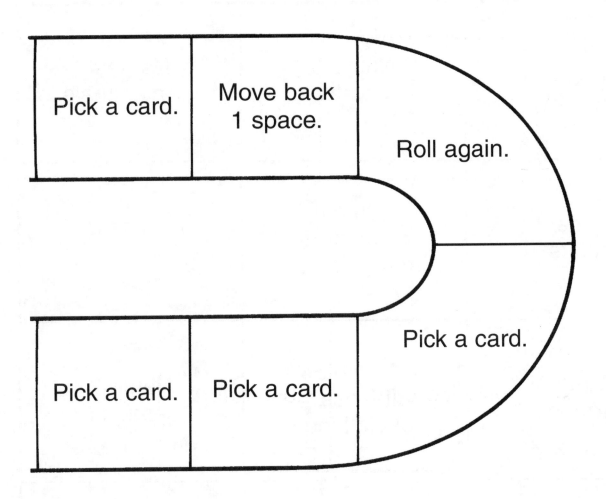

Pick a card.

Move back 1 space.

Roll again.

Pick a card.

Pick a card.

Pick a card.

Pick a card.

Move back 1 space.

End

Category Game Cards

Name 2 things you can write with.	Name 5 sports.	Name 4 farm animals.
Name 3 colors.	Name 4 characters from a book.	Name 2 stores.
Name 4 cartoons.	Name 5 pieces of clothing.	Name 2 seasons.
Name 4 months.	Name 3 jungle animals.	Name 2 tools.
Name 5 letters.	Name 3 numbers.	Name 3 teachers.

Category Game Cards (cont.)

Name 3 utensils.	Name 4 parts of the body.	Name 5 vehicles.
Name 4 fruits.	Name 4 vegetables.	Name 5 things you could find in a kitchen.
Name 2 things you can read.	Name 3 things you could find at the beach.	Name 4 things you turn on.
Name 3 things that hold other things.	Name 5 things that are blue.	Name 5 things in a classroom.
Name 5 things you can find outside.	Name 3 things that you can ride.	Name 2 things that are hot.

Categorize It

Directions: Cut out the word/picture cards at the bottom of the page. Glue the word/picture cards in the correct column.

Furniture	Vehicles	Tools

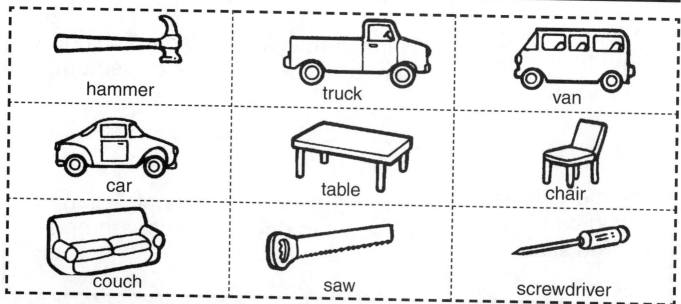

hammer   truck   van

car   table   chair

couch   saw   screwdriver

Categorize Food

Directions: Cut out the word/picture cards at the bottom of the page. Glue the word/picture cards in the correct boxes.

Fruits	Vegetables
Meats	**Breads**

bun	ham	broccoli	cherries
carrots	banana	muffin	peas
chicken	bagel	apple	steak

Categorize and Classify

Directions: Cut out the word/picture cards at the bottom of the page. Determine the two categories the objects fall into. Glue the word/picture cards by the categories. Classify the categories by labeling the columns at the top.

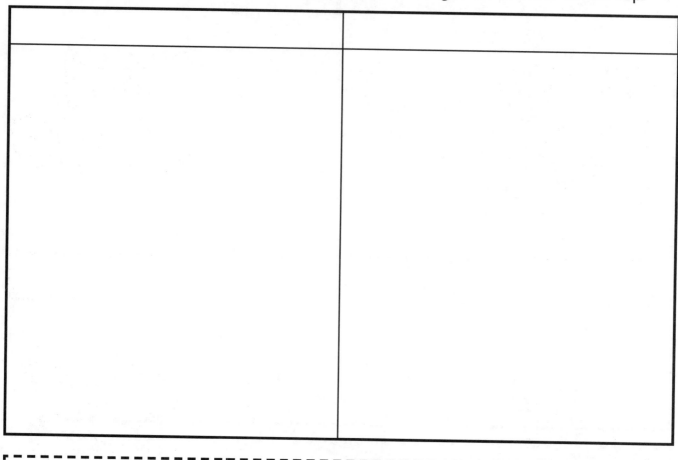

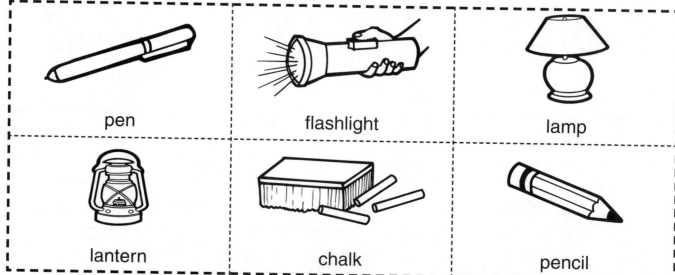

pen

flashlight

lamp

lantern

chalk

pencil

Classifying Objects

Directions: Cut out the word cards at the bottom of the page. Look at each group of objects. Determine the word card that best names each group of objects.

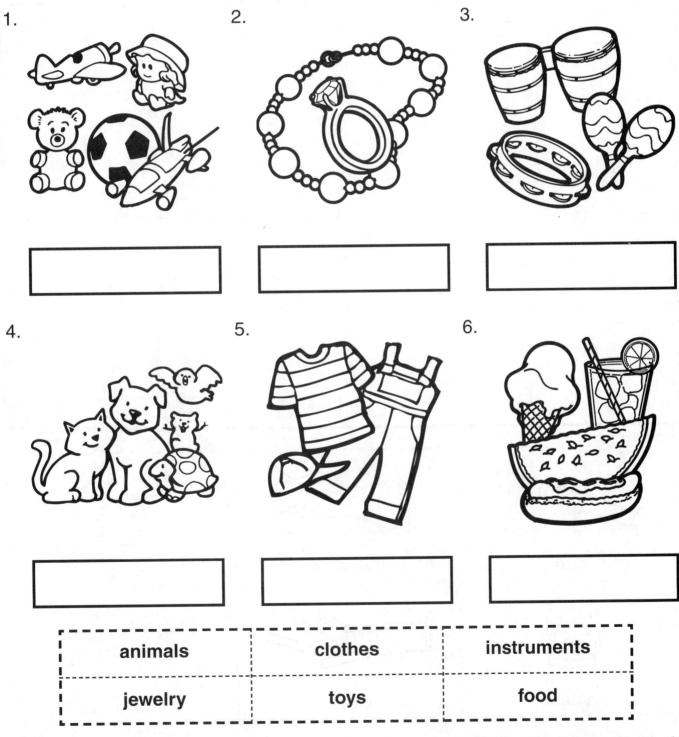

animals	clothes	instruments
jewelry	toys	food

Categorizing and Classifying

Directions: Cut out the word/picture cards at the bottom of the page. Determine four categories the objects fall into. Glue the word/picture cards by the categories. Classify the categories by labeling the boxes.

_____	_____
_____	_____

ice cream	horse	paints	cake
crayon	soccer ball	markers	football
tennis racket	cookies	cow	pig

Comprehension

Comprehension is at the crux of why we read. We read in order to gain meaning from a text. Thus, comprehension instruction is crucial to teaching reading. Good readers read for a variety of reasons: to follow a recipe or a sign, for directions, or to learn something from a book. Good readers read in order to derive meaning from a text for a purpose and/or for pleasure. They also actively participate while they are reading. They are engaged in gaining meaning from the text, and they develop strategies for maintaining their understanding when problems arise. Good reading instruction provides students with both a purpose to read and strategies for monitoring comprehension.

Because comprehension—gaining meaning from a text—is such a critical piece of reading, it is important to teach students how to monitor themselves when they are reading. Students need to know when their understanding of the text has broken down and ways they can resolve the comprehension problem. Good instruction in comprehension teaches students strategies they can use for monitoring comprehension and provides as practice in using those strategies on a variety of texts.

Researchers on reading have discovered many activities and strategies which expert readers employ when they are reading, such as: hypothesizing, rephrasing, seeking of relationships between ideas, and monitoring of breakdowns in comprehension. Good readers use these strategies freely and appropriately in order to derive meaning from a text. Many students are able to acquire these reading strategies without direct instruction. However, many students who may be able to decode text may not be able to comprehend what is being said. These students need direct, explicit instruction on how to gain meaning from text.

The reading comprehension section of this book provides activities and strategies that can be used with children to increase their comprehension, as well as to increase their understanding of the types of things they should be looking for when they read a text. The last few pages of this section provide some reading comprehension worksheets appropriate for first grade. These worksheets can be used to practice many of the strategies provided within this section.

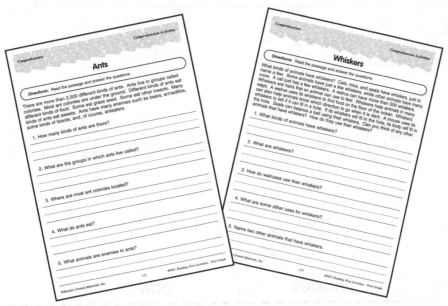

Reciprocal Teaching

Reciprocal teaching encourages students to interact with a text in order to construct meaning. Reciprocal teaching's basis is teaching and modeling reading strategies through structured and explicit instruction that will enable students to comprehend the text. The reading strategies taught are: questioning, summarizing, clarifying, and predicting. Students and teacher use these reading strategies in a dialog, which promotes students' interactions with text in order to construct meaning. The result of both the explicit teaching and modeling is that students are learning when and how to use these reading strategies to construct meaning.

The key benefit of reciprocal teaching is that it provides more than one strategy for students to use. It also helps build scaffolding which enable the student sufficient and appropriate support in order to be successful at negotiating the text. The teaching begins by overtly and explicitly teaching students the reading strategies of questioning, summarizing, clarifying, and predicting. The teacher then begins the lesson, carefully modeling each of the strategies during the course of the discussion about a text. Students are always active participants in the process; however, the degree to which they lead the discussion varies depending on how much support the students need during the discussion. In the beginning, the teacher is solely responsible for the discussion in order to model. Gradually, as students become more comfortable with the procedure, control of the discussion is given over to the students. Students are able to practice the strategies with the teacher monitoring the discussion in order to provide support to students or the discussion when needed. The ultimate goal is for students to internalize these strategies and to use them to self-monitor as they are reading. All four of the reading strategies included in reciprocal teaching serve as important tools students can use while negotiating the text in order to make meaning.

Questioning

The aim of teaching students to question is to help them identify main ideas in reading passages. The task of forming questions requires students to identify main ideas or information of significance in order to help ask good questions. Additionally, when students know that they will be forming questions at the end of reading a passage, it gives them a purpose for reading. The very act of questioning based on a passage requires students to become involved with the text in order to pose and answer questions. See page 157 for additional questioning activities.

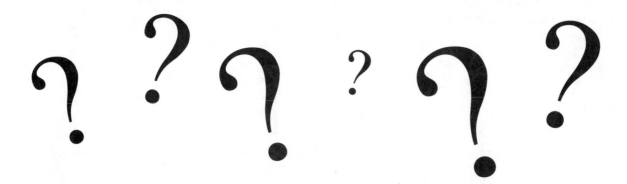

Reciprocal Teaching (cont.)

Summarizing

Summarizing is a quick method of finding out if a text has been completely understood. Summarizing requires students to integrate all of the information presented in the text by asking them to identify main ideas. It also helps students to identify significant events, organize concepts, and draw conclusions.

Clarifying

Clarifying helps students and teachers identify when there has been a breakdown in comprehension. It is an essential component because it gives the student permission to find the text confusing. Helping students identify strategies that can be used when they come across a confusing passage will help them self-monitor in order to increase comprehension. At times, a helpful strategy may be to simply reread the text. Other times, students may need to read on in order to have clarification. Of course, other strategies such as consulting a dictionary or another person are invaluable, too. By clarifying, students are taught to identify the reasons a text may be confusing to them, such as new vocabulary, or a new concept, and to be alert for the effects these have on comprehension. The key is to get students to stop and clarify the text instead of giving up or reading on without comprehension.

Predicting

The final reading strategy of prediction serves an important role in keeping students actively thinking while reading. As students hypothesize about what will happen next, expectations are created by which the student will want to continue to read. This creates a purpose for reading, as well as increasing meaning and memorability of the text. Predicting helps students make a connection between what they already know and the new knowledge they are gaining. A student's predictions also provide the teacher with information about the extent of a student's prior knowledge, as well as his comprehension of the text read thus far. Knowing the extent or lack of prior knowledge a student has enables the teacher to provide ways, such as language experience, to help the student gain knowledge that may help him or her to understand a text better.

Reciprocal Teaching (cont.)

Implementing Reciprocal Teaching

Essential to the teaching of reciprocal teaching is introducing the students to and modeling the four reading strategies. This can be done all at one time or on several days. In the beginning, the teacher assumes much of the responsibility of modeling how to use these four reading strategies with the text that is being read. Modeling is accomplished by the teacher thinking aloud and eliciting responses from students based on the questions generated. Students gradually begin practicing the strategies on small segments of text. The teacher still maintains much of the responsibility. Gradually, as students become more familiar with the four strategies and begin using them in the discussion, they take over the responsibility of the discussion by asking each other questions, summarizing, clarifying, and predicting. During the time that students are practicing each of the reading strategies, the teacher monitors the discussions in order to be sure the students are using the strategies correctly and have an understanding of the text.

There are many ways to scaffold instruction using reciprocal teaching. Listed below are several ways you may wish to consider.

✏ Student Pairs

Students can be paired and assigned responsibility for one of the strategies. For example, one pair would be responsible for generating questions, another pair would be responsible for summarizing, another pair responsible for clarifying, and the last pair would be responsible for predicting. Each student reads the text with his or her partner, and then together they prepare the portion for which they are responsible. At the end of an appointed time, the students come together with their ideas. A student leader begins the discussion by asking the group responsible for generating the questions. The remaining groups participate by discussing the questions with their partners. The format remains the same for the remaining strategies.

✏ Come With Questions

In this format, students read the material in class, sometimes silently and other times in groups, and come to the discussion with any questions, summaries, clarifications, and predictions they may have. A different student each day is selected to facilitate the discussion in which students participate by using their own prepared material or to answer or add to another student's response. The teacher's job is to monitor the discussion, pose new questions, and keep the discussion on track.

✏ One of Each

Once students are very familiar with each of the strategies, you may wish to have them come to a discussion with one question, one summary, one clarification, and one prediction. You can have students write down their ideas if desired. Conduct a whole-class discussion, or consider dividing the students into groups and assigning a leader for each group.

Questioning

You Write the Questions

This strategy works well with reciprocal teaching (see page 154). Before reading a passage, tell students that when they are done reading you want them to think of questions that could be asked about the text. Students need to come up with the questions. Other students or even the teacher can answer the questions. This technique also works well if you will be using a reading comprehension worksheet on which students are to write the answer to the question. Prior to distributing the activity sheet, have students generate a list of questions they think will be asked. Points or prizes can be distributed for each question that matches those on the activity sheet; however, that is not necessary. Students are often just thrilled that they thought of the question that appears on a worksheet. See pages 171–174 for examples of some reading comprehension worksheets.

Prove Your Answer

This technique can be used with reading comprehension worksheets, such as those found on pages 171–174, or by photocopying the page of text students have read out of a storybook or even a text book. Have students justify their answers to comprehension questions by locating the answer back in the text. Provide each student with a highlighter or have them use a yellow or orange crayon. While answering the comprehension questions, students must look back to the text, locate where the answer is found, and highlight the text. This is an excellent technique for inference questions in which the answer is not specifically stated in the text. Students must find other clues in the text that support their inferential answer.

Jeopardy

Reverse the roles of questions and answers. Think of several questions you would like students to be able to answer after reading a text. Once students have read the text, give them the answers to the questions. Students must come up with the question that corresponds with the answer you provided. This activity works well as an individual activity; however, students love to work together in order to complete this assignment.

All Questions Are Not Created Equal

Most teachers are familiar with the term "higher level thinking." Although we do want students to understand texts on a literal level, we want students to be thinking on other levels, too. A chart of the levels of Bloom's Taxonomy, as well as a list of key words to be used when formulating questions, is provided on page 158.

Using Bloom's Taxonomy

Questioning Level	Purpose	Key Questioning Words
Knowledge	recall learned information	define, describe, identify, label, list, match, name, recall, select, state
Comprehension	master basic understanding of information	summarize, describe, interpret, predict, estimate, classify, generalize, give examples, restate
Application	do something new with information	apply, demonstrate, solve, relate, classify, discover, calculate
Analysis	examine the parts of a whole	analyze, infer, compare, contrast, identify
Synthesis	to put together parts to create something new	combine, rearrange, plan, substitute, contrast, create
Evaluation	form and defend an opinion	assess, rank, grade, measure, judge, compare, conclude

Main Idea

Another Title

After students have read a text in its entirety, an excellent activity is for them to think of another title for the book. By renaming the book or reading passage, students must practice identifying the main idea of the book. In essence, students are summarizing the book with one or a few key words. Have several students offer alternative titles to the text. Chart student suggestions and then have the class vote on the best title. Include the real title as one of the options for which students can vote. Which title comes out the winner, the real title or a student title? Often the answer to that question is surprising.

Train Ride

Help students identify the main ideas of a text by completing the Train Ride template on page 160. After reading a text, ask students to identify the main idea of the text and the three most important details that support the main idea. Use the train pattern on page 160 to help visually organize the information. The main idea should go in the engine of the train. The three supporting details should be written in the cars of the train. If more supporting details are applicable, photocopy the train multiple times. Have students cut out the engine and as many train cars as are applicable. The train can be glued together on a separate sheet of construction paper. If appropriate to the text and the ability levels of your children, examples of the details or further description of the details can be written in the wheels of the train.

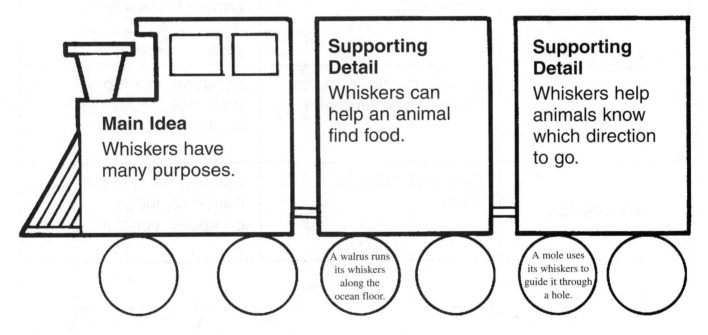

Main Idea
Whiskers have many purposes.

Supporting Detail
Whiskers can help an animal find food.

Supporting Detail
Whiskers help animals know which direction to go.

A walrus runs its whiskers along the ocean floor.

A mole uses its whiskers to guide it through a hole.

Train Ride

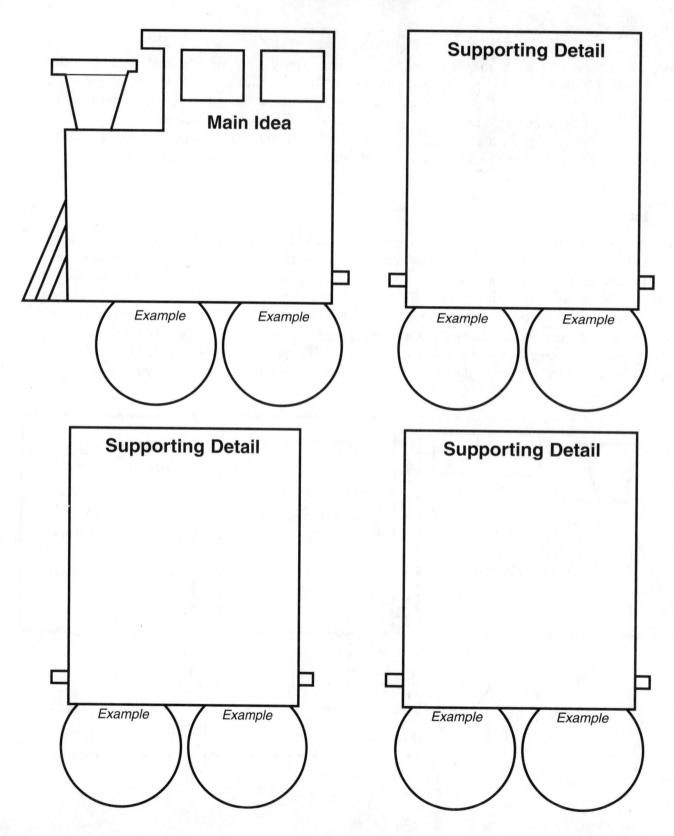

Main Idea

Example

Example

Supporting Detail

Example

Example

Supporting Detail

Example

Example

Supporting Detail

Example

Example

Making Inferences

Title Only

Draw on students' background knowledge and prior experiences prior to reading a text to students. Tell students the title of the book, but do not show them the cover yet. Ask students what they know about the topic or title. Create a word web to chart student comments and ideas. Often students bring a wealth of ideas to the conversation. Vocabulary from the book is often used by students during the discussion. Once students have had a chance to share, show students the cover of the book and ask them to make a prediction about the contents of the book. Chart students' comments, if appropriate. Then read the book to students. After the first reading of the book, return to the word web and circle any comments or vocabulary words that were applicable to the book.

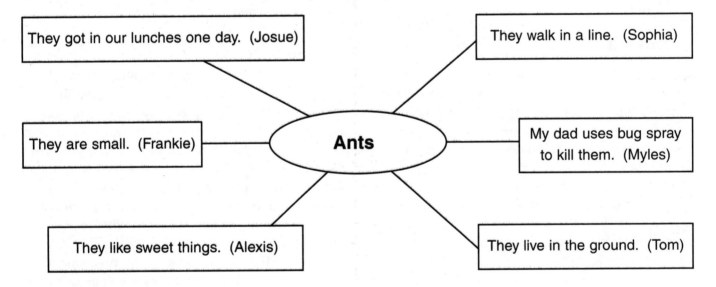

They got in our lunches one day. (Josue)

They walk in a line. (Sophia)

They are small. (Frankie)

Ants

My dad uses bug spray to kill them. (Myles)

They like sweet things. (Alexis)

They live in the ground. (Tom)

Mystery Object

This activity is excellent for helping students practice making inferences. Place a mystery object in a brown paper bag. Think of 3-5 clues that are appropriate for the mystery object. Tell the clues to the students, one clue at a time. See if students can guess the mystery object without being told the name of the object. For example, if the object in the bag was a leaf, the clues could be as follows:

1. The mystery object is green.

2. It grows on a tree.

3. Its color may change to red, orange, or brown.

4. It falls off the tree in the autumn.

Allow students to bring objects from home to place in the brown paper bag. Be sure to remind them to prepare 3–5 clues to offer as to the contents of the bag.

Visualizing

When good readers read, they create a picture in their minds of what is happening in the story. It is because of this picture that readers often "like the book better than the movie." This picture helps a reader understand the story better because they are keeping characters, setting, plot, and any other elements of a story straight in their head through the creation of this picture. When the picture becomes fuzzy, the reader knows he or she needs to go back and reread because comprehension has been lost.

Teaching students to learn to visualize a story or create a picture in their head can be a helpful comprehension tool. Helpful initial lessons in visualizing include drawing an image of what they hear from the text. Once students understand how to do an illustration showing their visualization, oral activities that encourage students to express what they are envisioning can be useful and less time consuming.

Illustrate It

Primary students are very dependent on the illustrations in a book in order to gain meaning. The pictures in most books help carry the meaning in the story. How many times have you been reading a story to your class when you hear the words, "I can't see the pictures." It is precisely that reason that this strategy works so well for students. Every once in a while read a story to students; however, do not show them the pictures that go with the book. You may want to warn them ahead of time that you will not be showing the pictures so you do not have disappointed students. Tell students that you want them to listen very carefully to the story because they are going to have to draw a picture about what is happening in the story. Then, read an appropriate portion of the book (this could be a page or two, half the book, or even the whole book) to students and have them draw an illustration about what is happening in the story. Once students are done with their pictures, reread the text to them. Have them look at their pictures to see if what they drew matches the text. Allow them to make any revisions if necessary. You may even want to show students the pictures from the book after they are done drawing so they can compare their illustrations.

Tell What You See

This strategy is similar to Illustrate It; however, rather than drawing a picture, students tell about what they are picturing in their heads. For example, if you are reading a story about a snowy day, encourage students to tell what that looks like. Students may say, "I see white everywhere I look. Icicles are hanging from the roof. Kids are out of school on a snow day. A group of children is building a snowman and other children are having a snowball fight." Be sure to use reading passages with which students will have had some previous experience, especially when beginning this activity. Also, be sure to model the activity so students have an idea what you are looking for when you are asking them to visualize.

Making Connections

A great reading strategy for students to use to increase comprehension is to make connections with prior knowledge or experiences. Encourage students to see and make connections by charting the connections that students find. By being reminded of similar experiences the student has had with the text, students are apt to remember other things that may increase comprehension of the text as well, especially vocabulary words and concepts. Additionally, students who have not had those same experiences will benefit from hearing another child talk about a similar situation.

Create two large charts out of chart paper and place in a prominent place in the classroom. Label one chart Text-To-Text Connections and label the other chart Text-To-Life Connections. Explain to students the purpose of each chart. An excellent time to explain the charts purpose is when you have a connection to make and can model the first one for each chart. Add to the appropriate chart each time students make a reading connection.

Text-to-Text Connections

Text-to-text connections are connections students see between the text currently being read and another text that has already been read. The student should state the name of each of the texts when listing his or her connection.

> When we read the story <u>There Was an Old Lady Who Swallowed a Bat</u>, it reminded me of the book <u>There Was an Old Lady Who Swallowed a Fly</u>. In both stories, a lady swallowed a lot of crazy things.

Text-to-Life Connections

Text-to-life connections are connections students make between the text currently being read and a previous life experience. The students should state the element of the text (such as the event, character, or even the setting) and the real-life experience of which the text element reminds him or her.

> When Ira spent the night at Reggie's house in the book <u>Ira Sleeps Over</u>, it reminded me about the time my friend Steffi spent the night at my house. We built a fort out of blankets and stayed up telling ghost stories.

Graphic Organizers

Graphic organizers are excellent tools to help students understand a text better. Graphic organizers help students sort important information from unimportant information. They also help break down the whole text into manageable pieces. Additionally, most graphic organizers show the relationship of those pieces to each other.

When completing graphic organizers, students often have to return to the text to locate information. Returning to the text with a set purpose helps build comprehension of the text. Additionally, students see important aspects of the text they should be noticing when reading it. It sets the stage for future readings. For example, if a student is completing a story map, such as the one found on page 166, and he does not remember the setting, he will have to return to the text in order to determine the setting. The setting is an important part of a story that good readers note when reading. When reading the next text, the student will likely pay attention to the significance of the setting in relationship to the story.

There are a wide variety of graphic organizers available to be used with a variety of types of texts. In fact, there are entire teacher resource books devoted to graphic organizers. Make use of them in order to help students understand important components of a text, as well as how those components work together in the text. Provided on pages 166–170 are four graphic organizers that can be used with a wide variety of texts read in the first grade. Remember, these graphic organizers can be reproduced on transparencies or recreated on chart paper and completed as a whole class activity. Using the graphic organizers as a whole-class activity is especially helpful in the beginning of the school year when most first-grade students would have a difficult time completing the writing or when introducing a new graphic organizer with which students are not yet familiar. See page 165 for a sample of each of the following graphic organizers.

✏ **Story Map**

The story map on page 166 is useful for showing the important elements of a story. The story map may be photocopied and used as is, or have students cut out the houses and glue them to a piece of construction paper in order to make a neighborhood scene. Encourage students to add a street, trees, and other details in order to complete the picture.

✏ **Sequencing**

The sequencing circles on page 167 and 168 can be used to show the sequence of events in a story, as well as to show the sequence of other events, such as the growing cycle of a tadpole/frog.

✏ **Causes and Effects**

The graphic organizer on page 169 is designed to show cause and effect relationships.

✏ **Classifying Information**

The graphic organizer titled Classifying Information on page 170 can be especially helpful to show relationships of items to each other. Although this organizer can be used with fiction texts, it is especially useful with nonfiction texts.

Graphic-Organizer Samples

Classifying Information

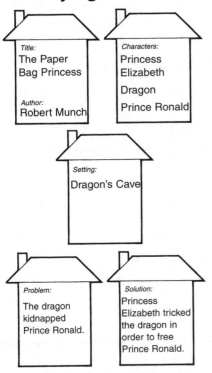

Title:
The Paper
Bag Princess

Author:
Robert Munch

Characters:
Princess
Elizabeth
Dragon
Prince Ronald

Setting:
Dragon's Cave

Problem:
The dragon
kidnapped
Prince Ronald.

Solution:
Princess
Elizabeth tricked
the dragon in
order to free
Prince Ronald.

Sequencing

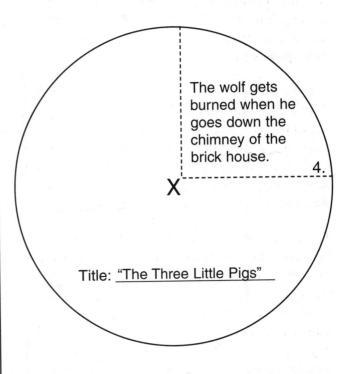

The wolf gets burned when he goes down the chimney of the brick house.

X   4.

Title: "The Three Little Pigs"

Cause and Effects Organizer

Cause: Give a mouse a cookie. → *Effect:* He will want milk to go with it.

Cause: Give a mouse some paper and crayons. → *Effect:* He will want to hang his picture on the refrigerator.

Cause: When the mouse sees the refrigerator. → *Effect:* He will become thirsty and ask for something to drink.

Classifying Information

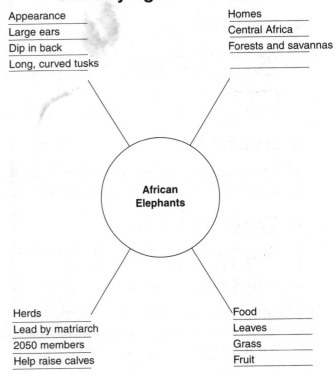

Appearance
Large ears
Dip in back
Long, curved tusks

Homes
Central Africa
Forests and savannas

African Elephants

Herds
Lead by matriarch
2050 members
Help raise calves

Food
Leaves
Grass
Fruit

Story Map

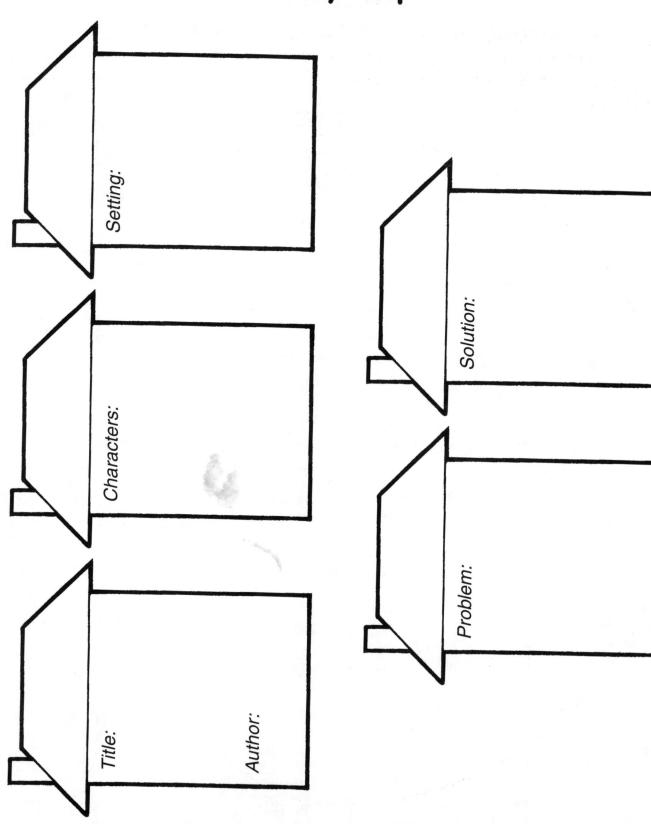

Setting:

Characters:

Title:

Author:

Solution:

Problem:

Sequencing

Directions: Photocopy pages 167 and 168 onto index paper. Illustrate the sequence of the story in the four pie shapes on page 168. Cut out the circles on both pages. Attach the two pages using a brad. Spin the top piece to show the sequence of the text.

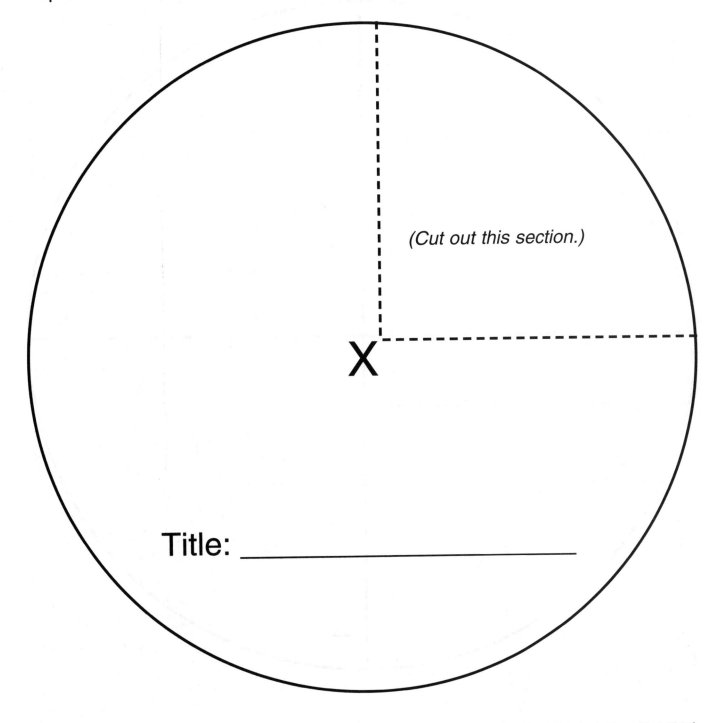

(Cut out this section.)

X

Title: _____

Sequencing (cont.)

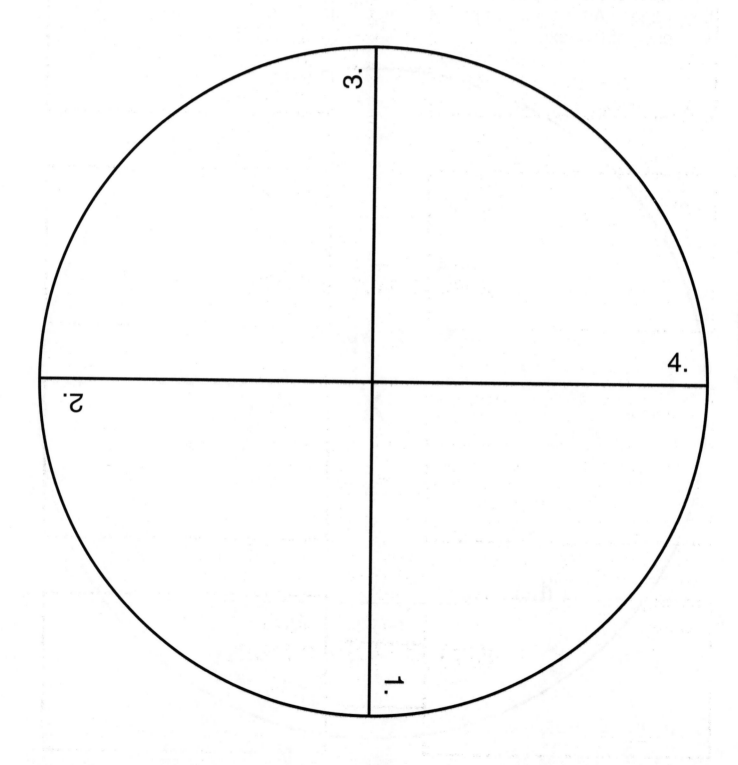

Cause and Effects Organizer

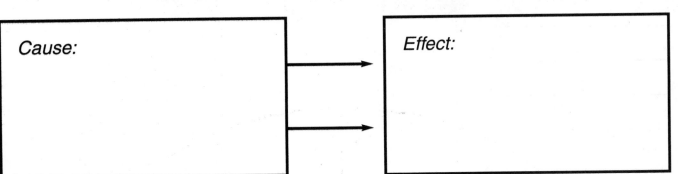

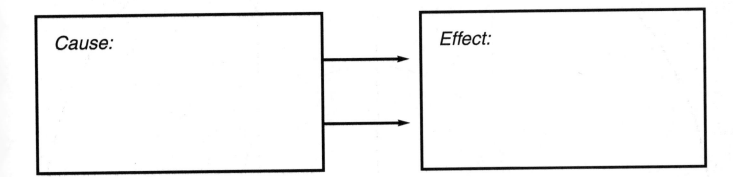

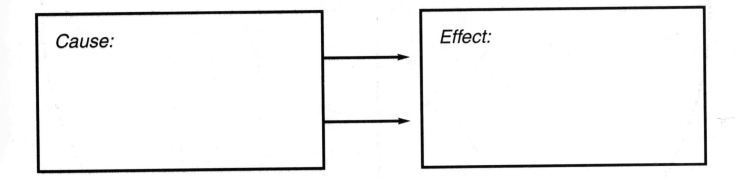

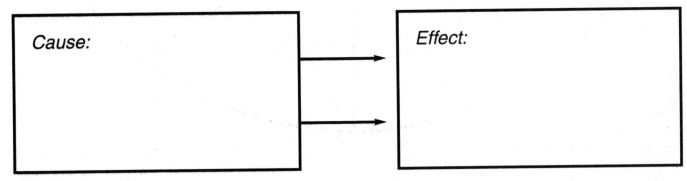

Classifying Information Organizer

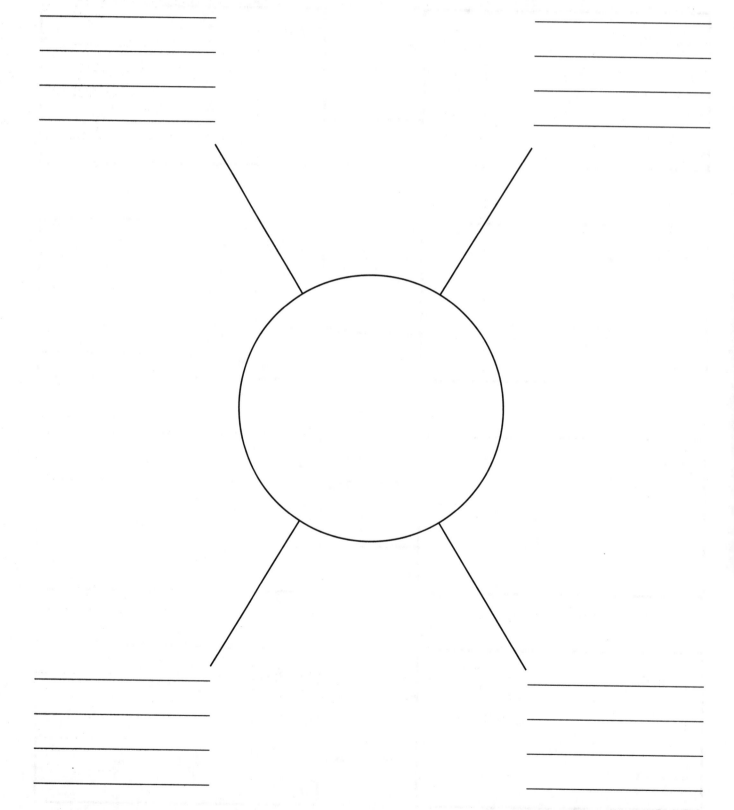

Ants

> **Directions:** Read the passage and answer the questions.

There are more than 2,500 different kinds of ants. Ants live in groups called colonies. Most ant colonies are under the ground. Different kinds of ants eat different kinds of food. Some eat grass seed. Some eat other insects. Many kinds of ants eat sweets. Ants have many enemies such as bears, armadillos, some kinds of lizards, and, of course, anteaters.

1. How many kinds of ants are there?

_____

_____

2. What are the groups in which ants live called?

_____

_____

3. Where are most ant colonies located?

_____

_____

4. What do ants eat?

_____

_____

5. What animals are enemies to ants?

_____

_____

Cactus

Directions: Read the passage and answer the questions.

Cactuses grow in places where it does not rain much. When it does rain, their roots get as much water as they can. A cactus can store water for many years. There are more than 2,000 kinds of cactuses. Cactuses come in many different shapes and sizes. Some cactuses are tall and thin. Others cactuses are short and round. Cactuses have spines instead of leaves. Many cactus spines are very sharp.

1. Where do cactus grow?

_____

- -

_____

2. What do cactus do when it rains?

_____

- -

_____

3. How many kinds of cactus are there?

_____

- -

_____

4. What are some of the shapes and sizes of cactus?

_____

- -

_____

5. What do cactus have instead of leaves?

_____

- -

_____

Whiskers

Directions: Read the passage and answer the questions.

What kinds of animals have whiskers? Cats, mice, and seals have whiskers, just to name a few. Some animals have just a few whiskers, while other animals have many more. A cat just has a few whiskers. A walrus can have more than 500 whiskers. Whiskers are hairs that an animal can use to feel. Whiskers help animals in many ways. A walrus uses its whiskers to find food on the floor of the ocean. Whiskers can also help animals know which direction to go when it is dark. A mouse uses its whiskers to tell if it can fit in a hole. If its whiskers will fit in the hole, its body will fit in the hole. Seals can balance a ball using their whiskers. Can you think of any other animals that have whiskers? How do they use their whiskers?

1. What kinds of animals have whiskers?

_____

_____

2. What are whiskers?

_____

_____

3. How do walruses use their whiskers?

_____

_____

4. What are some other uses for whiskers?

_____

_____

5. Name two other animals that have whiskers.

_____

Black Bears

Directions: Read the passage and answer the questions.

Did you know black bears can be black, brown, or gray? Even though their colors may be different, they all have some things that are the same. Black bears have small heads and tan noses. Black bears are the smallest of all the kinds of bears there are. They even have small claws. Their small claws are good for climbing trees. Black bears hibernate in the winter. One of their favorite places to hibernate is in a hollow log. Black bears eat onions, honey, and ants. When they can find berries, black bears like to eat berries, too.

1. What color are black bears?

_____

- -

_____

2. What do black bears look like?

_____

- -

_____

3. Why can black bears climb trees so well?

_____

- -

_____

4. Where do black bears like to hibernate for the winter?

_____

- -

_____

5. What do black bears eat?

_____

- -

_____

Answer Key

Page 20
The pen, pot, pig, and pin should be glued in a box together. The map, man, mop, and mitt should be glued in a box together.

Page 21
1. log
2. tub
3. mop
4. sun
5. hat
6. sad
7. bell
8. stick

Page 22
Short a—jam, hat, map
Short e—pen, jet, bed
Short o—log, pot, sock

Page 27
1. fan
2. mat
3. net
4. pig
5. mop
6. hat

Page 28
1. sock
2. ball
3. jam
4. ten
5. pin
6. bun

Page 29
1. jet
2. pot
3. log
4. pan
5. map
6. pig

Page 50
Small version of the page with answers shown on it.

Page 52
Small version of the page with answers shown on it.

Page 53
Begins with Dd—dot and dog
Begins with Jj—jam and jet
Begins with Qq—queen and quilt

Page 54
1. can
2. pan
3. sun
4. run
5. pin
6. fin
7. log
8. dog
9. pen
10. ten
11. hat
12. cat

Page 55
Ends with Nn—fan and pen
Ends with Pp—lip and map
Ends with Tt—rat and jet

Page 56
1. dog
2. dot
3. tub
4. tug
5. pin
6. pig
7. hat
8. ham
9. can
10. cat
11. sun
12. sub

Page 60
Cr—crown, crab
Dr—drum, dress
Gr—grass, grapes
Fr—frog, frown

Page 61
Sw—swim and swing
St—star and stick
Sk—skunk and skate
Sp—spider and spoon

Page 74
-ap—cap, tap, map
-at—bat, cat, rat
-an—fan, can, man
-ag—wag, tag, bag

Page 75
Answers will vary.

Page 76
Answers will vary.

Page 77
1. hop
2. hot
3. lock
4. jog
5. pop
6. cot

Page 78
-un—bun, run, sun
-ug—bug, jug, hug
-ub—tub, cub, sub

Page 118
Show a small version of the page with answers on it.

Page 119
ill, sick
pretty, beautiful
go, leave
cry, weep
thrilled, excited
nice, kind

Page 120
1. shut
2. bucket
3. hurry
4. speak
5. angry
6. quiet
7. start
8. small

Page 121
1. young
2. sour
3. out
4. walk
5. sad
6. closed
7. small
8. cold

Page 122
1. empty
2. hard
3. laugh
4. young
5. white
6. down
7. moon
8. small

Page 123
1. start, end
2. grin, frown
3. weep, laugh
4. shut, open
5. angry, happy
6. above, under

Page 124

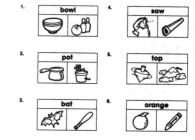

Page 125
1. can
2. play
3. left
4. cold
5. cold
6. play
7. left
8. can

Page 126
1. doctor
2. firefighter
3. chef
4. police officer
5. teacher
6. construction worker
7. mail carrier
8. crossing guard
9. sanitation worker

Page 127
1. ship
2. car
3. airplane
4. train
5. spaceship
6. bus
7. motorcycle
8. truck

Page 128
1. igloo
2. hut
3. house
4. tipi
5. apartment
6. castle

Page 129
1. swimsuit
2. top
3. sneakers
4. trousers
5. jacket
6. frock
7. pullover
8. sleepwear

Answer Key

Page 130
1. neighborhood
2. hospital
3. museum
4. school
5. department store
6. post office
7. grocery store
8. fire station
9. bank

Page 131
1. river
2. island
3. ocean
4. lake
5. hill
6. mountain

Page 132
1. bald eagle
2. Statue of Liberty
3. Liberty Bell
4. American flag
5. Lincoln Memorial
6. Washington Monument

Page 133
Town: apartment, store, taxi, garage
Country: cow, barn, tractor, pig

Page 134

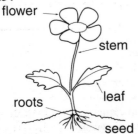

flower
stem
roots
leaf
seed

Page 135

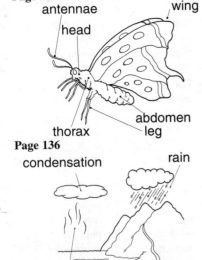

antennae
wing
head
thorax
abdomen
leg

Page 136
condensation
rain
evaporation
run-off

Page 137
Solid: book, table
Liquid: glass of water, pond
Gas: balloon, tire

Page 138
Feathers: hummingbird, eagle
Fur: tiger, bear
Scales: fish, snake

Page 139
1. balance
2. thermometer
3. rule
4. scale
5. meter stick
6. clock

Page 140
1. cylinder
2. pyramid
3. sphere
4. rectangular prism
5. cone
6. cube

Page 142
1. flute
2. tuba
3. clarinet
4. violin
5. trumpet
6. guitar
7. drums
8. trombone
9. piano

Page 148
Furniture: table, chair, couch
Vehicles: truck, van, car
Tools: hammer, screwdriver, saw

Page 149
Fruits: cherries, banana, apple
Vegetables: carrots, broccoli, peas
Meats: fish, steak, chicken
Breads: bun, muffin, bagel

Page 150
The pen, chalk, and pencil should be grouped together and labeled "Writing."
The lantern, flashlight, and lamp should be grouped together and labeled "Lighting."

Page 151
1. toys
2. jewelry
3. instruments
4. animals
5. clothing
6. food

Page 152
Desserts: ice cream, cake, cookies
Animals: horse, cow, pig
Sports: tennis, football, soccer
Art Tools: crayon, markers, paints

Page 171
1. There are more than 2,500 kinds of ants.
2. Ants live in groups called colonies.
3. Ant colonies are located underground.
4. Ants eat grass seed, insects, and sweets.
5. Bears, lizards, and anteaters are enemies to ants.

Page 172
1. Cactus grow where there is not much rain.
2. When it rains, they store water.
3. There are more than 2,000 kinds of cactuses.
4. Cactus can be tall and thin or short and round.
5. Cactus have spines.

Page 173
1. Cats, mice, walruses, and seals have whiskers.
2. Whiskers are hairs that help an animal feel.
3. Walrus use their whiskers to find food.
4. Accept any answer that is in the paragraph.
5. Accept any answer that is appropriate.

Page 174
1. Black bears can be black, brown, or gray.
2. Black bears have small heads and tan noses.
3. Black bears have small claws.
4. Black bears hibernate in hollow logs.
5. Black bears eat onions, honey, ants, and berries.